WEATHER EXPERIMENTS BOOK FOR KIDS

WEATHER EXPERIMENTS

BOOK FOR KIDS

MORE THAN 25 HANDS-ON ACTIVITIES TO LEARN ABOUT RAIN, WIND, HURRICANES, AND MORE

Jessica Stoller-Conrad

ROCKRIDGE
PRESS

For Tim, Freddie, and Felix, who bring sunshine
on even the cloudiest of days.

Interior and Cover Designer: Julie Schrader
Art Producer: Tom Hood
Editor: Barbara J. Isenberg
Production Editor: Emily Sheehan
Production Manager: Jose Olivera

Illustrations © Stuart Holmes, 2021, supplemental illustration courtesy of Shutterstock, pp ii, iv, viii, 1, 6, 8, 9, 27, 49, 90, 91, 103, 127. Photographs courtesy of Nikolay Vinokurov/Alamy, p. 4; SPL/Alamy, p. 14; Gregory K. Scott/Science Source, p. 22; Art Wolfe/Science Source, p. 23; Georg Gerster/Science Source, p. 24; SPL/Science Source pp 25, 54; Michael Nolan/Science Source, p. 53; Shutterstock, pp 55, 119; Andreas Thaller/Alamy, p. 69; John A. Ey III/Science Source, p. 70; Image Broker/Alamy, p. 71; Science History Images/Science Source, p. 81; NSF/Alamy, p. 81; Signal Photos/Alamy, p. 81; Ryan McGinnis/Alamy, p. 95. Author photo courtesy of Chelsea Mason.

Paperback ISBN: 978-1-63807-509-7 | eBook ISBN: 978-1-63878-010-6
R0

CONTENTS

WELCOME TO THE WORLD OF WEATHER!

You're enjoying a sunny morning at the beach, but by noon it's a rainy mess. Or you're wearing a T-shirt and shorts to school one day—but a week later, you're shivering in a heavy coat. Dealing with our planet's weather can be tricky.

Even if it seems that weather just changes randomly, there are scientific reasons behind these weather patterns. In this book, you'll learn everything about the weather you see and hear about every day.

Growing up in Indiana, I experienced the weather extremes of all four seasons, which led me to ask lots of questions. Like what's the difference between a regular thunderstorm and one that makes tornadoes? Or why can some snow be packed into a ball, but other snow just flakes apart?

Scientists spend a lot of time looking at the world and asking questions, too. As I got older, I decided that I wanted to become a scientist. Eventually, I became a science writer—a person who explains what science teaches us about how the world works. This book contains easy-to-understand explanations of weather events, sometimes called weather phenomena. (A single event is a **weather phenomenon**.) But you won't just read about a weather phenomenon; you'll perform experiments to see for yourself how and why it happens. There is no better way to learn science than to do it yourself!

In each chapter, you'll find different types of experiments to help you learn the science behind a weather event. "Quick Query" experiments can be done in a few minutes, while "Observation Deck" experiments explore a concept more deeply. Some chapters even have "Take It Outside" experiments, where you'll use the actual weather outside to learn something new.

I'll guide you to approach the experiments the way a real scientist would, by using the **scientific method**. This is a process—or set of steps—that scientists follow when they try to answer questions about things we don't yet understand. Make an observation. Ask a question. Form a **hypothesis**. Make a prediction. Then perform your experiment to see what happens. These are steps in the scientific method.

The experiments don't involve special equipment or materials that are expensive or hard to find. Most supplies you'll need are things you probably have around the house, and you can find the rest at a grocery or craft store. Step-by-step instructions make it easy to follow along.

Be sure to read the "Caution" sections in each experiment.

 This section will warn if any materials can be dangerous and if you need special equipment or a grown-up lab partner to help you stay safe during the experiment.

Throughout the book, you'll see boldface words. These are terms that are important for budding scientists to understand. You'll find the scientific terms listed with their definitions in the glossary at the back of this book. You will also find plenty of space to jot down your notes on the experiments and your weather observations.

So, are you ready to find out what a low-pressure zone is? And if it will affect your plans to throw your birthday party at the park in a few days? Let's dig in and find out!

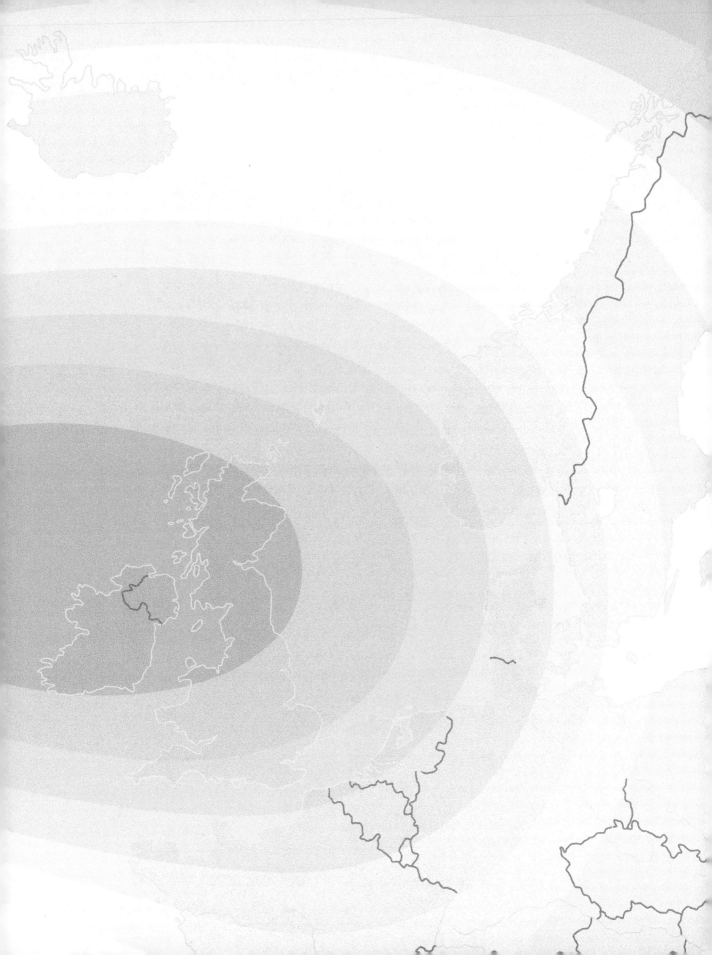

PART ONE

WEATHER

BASICS

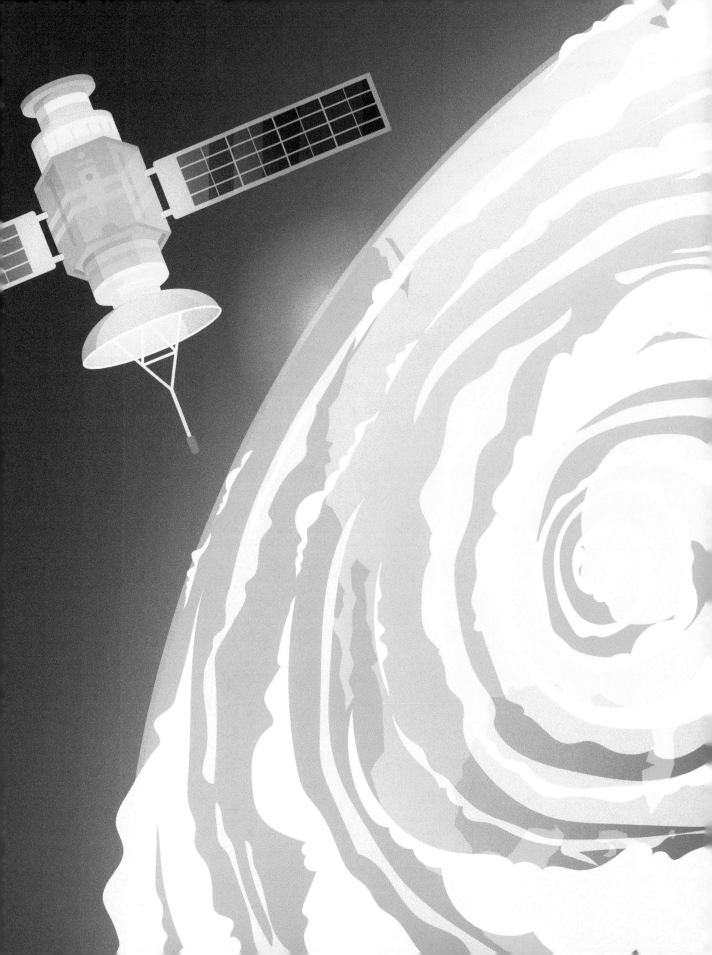

CHAPTER 1

WEATHER OR NOT?

A weather phenomenon is a natural event that is caused by a specific interaction among water, the **atmosphere**—the layers of gases and particles that surround our planet—and the land. Is it cloudy? Windy? Rainy? These are all examples of weather phenomena. In this chapter, we'll talk about what weather is—and what it isn't.

What Is a Weather Phenomenon?

We mostly talk about the weather when it's unpleasant or ruins our plans or sometimes when we see news about a natural disaster, such as a hurricane or tornado. But even when we're not thinking about it, weather is always happening all around us.

When it comes to weather, there is no such thing as an ordinary day. Even when it's mild outside and you don't notice anything remarkable, the oceans and the atmosphere are full of activity you can't see.

There may be no ordinary weather days, but in every region there are typical weather days in each season. If you live in Michigan, a typical winter day might mean freezing temperatures with snow and ice. If you live in Florida, though, a winter day is likely to be much warmer and milder.

No matter where you are, the atmosphere miles above you is constantly changing, and it can quickly change the weather along with it.

Rainstorm

What Is a Natural Disaster?

We've all had times when bad weather changed our plans for the day. But weather can be much, much worse. When weather events destroy homes, roads, and cities, it completely changes the lives of the people who live nearby. A devastating weather phenomenon like this is considered a **natural disaster**.

Hurricanes, floods, **wildfires**, and droughts are all types of weather-related natural disasters. These events can cause shortages of things that people need, such as housing, food, and medical care. Every year, close to 160 million people are affected by natural disasters.

Unfortunately, we can't prevent weather-related natural disasters from happening. But meteorologists have studied these weather events and can help give us a heads-up when they are likely to happen.

Weather, Climate, or Atmosphere?

Weather describes the conditions in Earth's atmosphere at a certain place and time. Weather is temporary—it changes all the time. Heat, rain, snow, and wind are all kinds of weather.

Climate describes the average weather conditions in a region over decades, centuries, or even longer. To describe a region's climate, we might say how hot or cold it is in different seasons or how much rain or snow falls.

Weather changes from day to day, or even hour to hour, but climate stays about the same from year to year.

Weather and climate have one important thing in common: Earth's atmosphere. Changes in weather are almost always a result of changes in the atmosphere. Changes in Earth's climate have to do with the atmosphere, too.

Weather is affected by the gas molecules that make up the air we breathe. The atmosphere is composed of nitrogen, oxygen, and other gases. There are billions of molecules of these gases in our atmosphere. Even though they are far too tiny for us to see, the weight of all those molecules adds up. We refer to how heavily the air is pushing down toward Earth's surface as **air pressure**.

Because the molecules are not evenly distributed, there can be large differences in air pressure that affect the weather. In areas of high pressure, the gas molecules in the atmosphere push down so strongly that clouds can't form. In areas of low pressure, the air isn't nearly as heavy. This means clouds can form, bringing rain and snow with them.

Climate is also affected by Earth's atmosphere, but in a different way.

Greenhouses are glass buildings that people use to grow plants that need warmth without using a powered heater. The glass walls and roof allow the Sun's rays to shine in, but they keep the Sun's heat from leaving, making the inside warmer.

Certain gases in our atmosphere also trap the Sun's heat. This phenomenon is called the **greenhouse effect**. Like the glass walls of a greenhouse, **greenhouse gases** in our atmosphere allow the Sun's rays to shine in, then trap its heat inside, warming Earth's surface.

Earth needs greenhouse gases—they are essential to life! Without them, Earth would be too cold and crops would be unable to grow. However, we need the right balance of these gases in our atmosphere. Too many greenhouse gases would make Earth too hot.

Unfortunately, many human activities, such as burning gasoline in a car engine or coal in a power plant, increase the amount of greenhouse gases in our atmosphere. These extra greenhouse gases are causing our planet to warm up more than it would naturally. This **global warming** can have very complicated effects.

As Earth warms, the atmosphere and oceans warm, too. Rising global average temperatures can cause changes in weather patterns across the planet. We call this **climate change**. For example, scientists predict that extreme weather—such as heat waves and large storms—will become more frequent or intense as these temperatures rise.

ALL ABOUT METEOROLOGY

Meteorology is the field of science that involves studying our atmosphere, how it changes, and how it affects our weather. A person who studies meteorology is called a meteorologist. These scientists collect and analyze information about the atmosphere and oceans to understand how changes in the water and sky will affect our weather.

Meteorologists begin by making observations. Of course they look outside to see what's happening right now, but that doesn't give them enough information to forecast what will happen with the weather. They also use tools to collect information.

For example, meteorologists use information collected from weather stations to help make their forecasts. A **weather station** is made up of several types of instruments that are constantly collecting information about the weather in a specific area. Weather stations are set up all over the world to measure temperature, air pressure, wind speed, humidity, and rainfall.

Meteorologists also get clues from the sky using instruments on research airplanes and weather satellites. **Weather satellites** are machines that orbit high above Earth, collecting information about the temperature, gases, water vapor, and clouds in our atmosphere.

Together, all this information helps meteorologists figure out weather forecasts for your area. Forecasts can help you decide if tomorrow will be a good day for a picnic or warn you that you'll need to seek safety during a storm. Most forecasts are good predictors of what to expect, and advance warnings of severe weather often help people save their property—and even their lives!

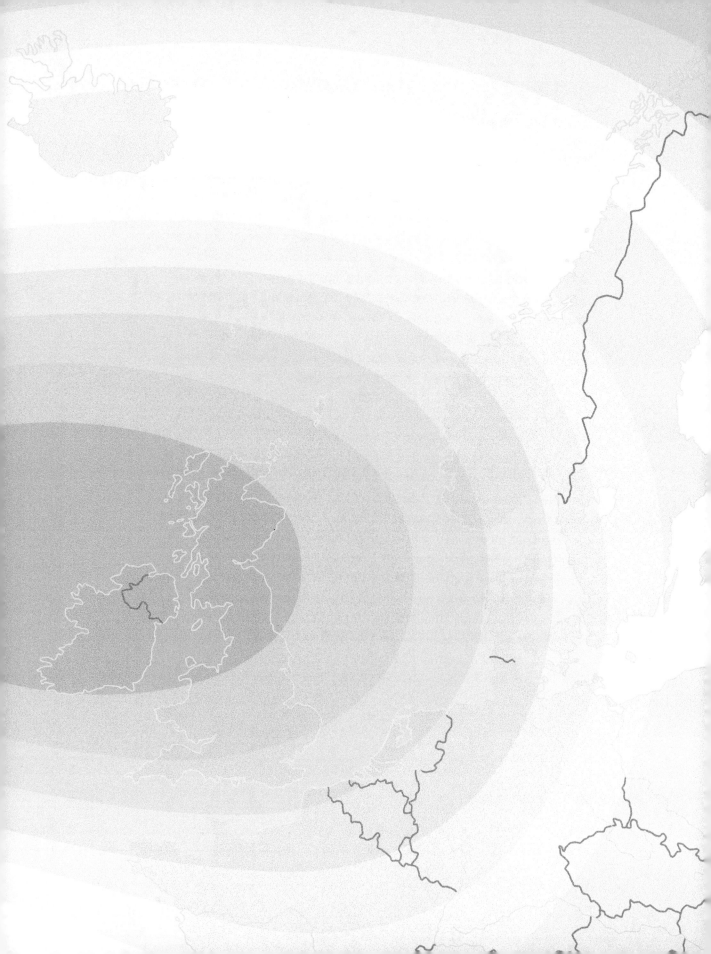

PART TWO
WEATHER
PHENOMENA

CHAPTER 2

WIND

Have you ever felt a gentle breeze on your face? Or seen a pile of leaves drift down the street? Thanks to Earth's atmosphere, we're surrounded by air all the time. But you might not even notice that it's there if it weren't for wind.

Wind is moving air. In general, wind happens when warm air rises and cool air rushes in to replace it. So where's the best place to find wind? It's very common to see windy conditions on the coasts of large bodies of water, such as oceans and lakes. The warm afternoon sun heats up the air near the coast, causing it to rise. And when that happens, cool air from above the water blows in to replace it. These winds are called sea breezes and lake breezes.

How Does It Do That?

Wind is caused by differences in air temperature and pressure. How does this work? Well, it all starts with the Sun.

1. **The Sun heats the Earth.** Because of how Earth is tilted on its axis, the Sun heats Earth unevenly. This creates patches of warmer and cooler air in our atmosphere.

2. **Warm air rises upward.** Warm air is less dense, or heavy, than cool air, so it rises upward. As these air molecules rise, they're no longer pushing down heavily on Earth's surface below. This creates an area of low air pressure beneath the patch of warm air.

3. **Air flows from areas of high pressure to areas of low pressure.** As warm air moves up, denser, cooler air rushes in to take its place. This movement of air creates wind.

4. **The Earth is constantly spinning on its axis.** As wind above Earth's surface rushes from areas of high pressure to areas of low pressure, the planet underneath all that air is still rotating, causing winds above Earth's surface to change direction slightly. This interaction between the spinning Earth and the atmosphere is called the **Coriolis effect**.

5. **Which way does the wind blow?** An east wind means there is a wind blowing from east to west. A west wind blows from west to east.

6. **A mighty wind.** The winds you see blowing in trees near the ground are called surface winds. But winds can be found much higher in the atmosphere, too. Five to nine miles above Earth's surface are **jet streams**: bands of strong winds that blow west to east across the globe. Jet streams travel at more than 100 miles per hour and can transport storms and other weather systems across the country.

TO THE EXTREMES!

Antarctica is widely considered to be the windiest place on Earth. Although other places have occasionally had stronger wind gusts, the average maximum daily wind speed in Cape Denison, Antarctica, is 44 miles (71 kilometers) per hour—and gusts of wind can reach more than 200 miles per hour! Cape Denison is also very cold, with temperatures often reaching far below 0°F (–18°C) in the winter.

Can a human survive in this harsh environment? Yes! Researchers actually live in canvas tents at Cape Denison to perform studies. Although human researchers are usually only temporary visitors, many penguins make windy Cape Denison their permanent home.

Jet streams, which travel at more than 100 miles per hour, can transport storms and other weather systems across the country. They can even help an airplane travel from Los Angeles to New York in much less time than it takes to make the return trip.

As the warming Earth causes climate change, the jet streams are changing—which also changes the weather. The North and South Poles are warming faster than other regions on Earth. This means that the temperature differences between the poles and the equator are not as dramatic as they once were, leading to weaker jet streams.

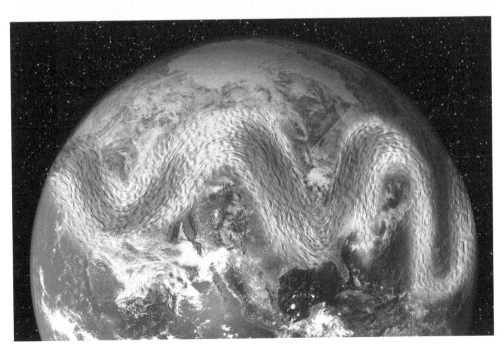

UP, UP, AND AWAY?

You've probably seen it in movies like *Up* . . . but is it really true? Could a house really be lifted up by a bunch of balloons? And how many balloons would it take?

The answer is a little complicated. After all, it depends on the size of the balloons, the size of the house, and whether or not the house is fastened to a foundation in the ground. Regardless of the details, it would take a lot of balloons to lift a house. Technicians at Pixar were said to have estimated that in real life, it would take 23.5 million helium balloons to lift the 1,800-square-foot house in the movie *Up*.

Although no one has tried this exact experiment, people have flown with helium balloons in real life many times. In fact, the activity even has a name: cluster ballooning.

Get Involved!

Ready to get swept away? In the experiments up next, we'll build a device to predict when big winds might be coming and figure out what the wind in your area is carrying.

Air pressure is important in the formation of wind, as air moves from areas of high pressure to areas of low pressure. The first experiment will teach you how to make a **barometer**—an instrument used to measure air pressure. You'll be able to use it to track changes in air pressure where you live. These readings can help you predict whether wind and storms might be on the way.

We'll go outside for the second wind experiment, where you'll learn exactly what is in the wind. Although the air we breathe is mostly made up of nitrogen, oxygen, and a few other gases, particles such as smoke, pollen, and dust are floating around in the atmosphere, too. In this experiment, you'll create a sticky trap to collect and analyze these particles—called **aerosols**—that are carried by the wind.

Now let's get ready to see air pressure and wind in action!

Pressure's On: Make Your Own Barometer

  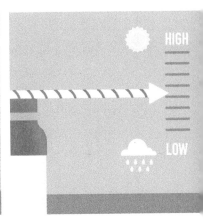

OBSERVATION DECK

The Big Idea: A drop in air pressure can mean a storm—and strong winds—are on the way. In this experiment, you'll make a barometer, which is an instrument used to detect local changes in the atmospheric pressure. If it's a nice day outside, what do you predict your barometer reading will be?

 Cautions: Have an adult lab partner help you with the superglue. Be careful to follow all directions on the package, and don't let the glue make contact with your skin.

MATERIALS:

- ☐ **Scissors**
- ☐ **Latex balloon**
- ☐ **1-quart jar**
- ☐ **Rubber band**
- ☐ **Superglue**

- ☐ **Paper or plastic straw**
- ☐ **Arrow cut out of paper**
- ☐ **Tape**
- ☐ **Paper or card stock**
- ☐ **Pen or pencil**

continued >

THE STEPS:

1. Find a good spot for your experiment. A table next to a wall will work nicely.

2. Use the scissors to snip off the neck of the balloon. Cut it at the spot where the narrow neck meets the circular body of the balloon. Discard the neck of the balloon.

3. Stretch the remaining body of the balloon over the top of the 1-quart jar. Use the rubber band to secure the balloon around the mouth of the jar.

4. Put a dot of superglue on the end of the straw and place it so that the glued end is attached to the middle of the balloon. The other end of the straw should hang over the edge of the jar.

5. Insert the non-pointed end of the paper arrow into the hollow end of the straw that is hanging off the edge of the jar. The pointed end of the arrow will indicate the level of the atmospheric pressure.

6. Tape the piece of paper on the wall next to the table. Place your jar next to the paper and draw a line at the level where the pointer is. Draw a line slightly above the pointer and label it "high." Draw a line slightly below the pointer and label it "low."

7. Record the position of the pointer in the following data table once or twice a day. As you record the barometer reading, record what the weather is like as well. Look at a weather forecasting app or website and also record what weather is expected in the next 24 hours.

Observations: What was the weather like when your barometer showed low atmospheric pressure? What about when the atmospheric pressure was high?

The Hows and Whys: When the atmospheric pressure is high, the weight of the gases in the atmosphere pushes down on Earth's surface. So when there's high air pressure, the gases push down heavily on the center of the balloon, causing the pointer to move up. When the air pressure is low, the gases in the jar begin to drift up. This causes the center of the balloon to move up and the pointer to move down. Low pressure can mean rainy weather is on the way. High pressure is often associated with mild or cold weather.

KICK IT UP A NOTCH: **Want a more precise barometer reading? Instead of just marking "high" and "low" above and below the initial reading, assign a number scale to your barometer. For example, you could draw five lines labeled 1 through 5 above the pointer and five lines labeled −1 through −5 below the pointer.**

	DAY 1	DAY 2	DAY 3	DAY 4	DAY 5
AIR PRESSURE: MORNING					
AIR PRESSURE: AFTERNOON					

Particle Catchers

TAKE IT OUTSIDE

The Big Idea: The wind blowing around outside is more than just air—lots of fine particles, called aerosols, are also carried by the wind. In this experiment, you'll make simple devices to catch and analyze particles blowing in the air around your neighborhood. You'll collect particles from several different spots.

 Cautions: None! This activity is safe for all ages.

MATERIALS:

- ☐ **Tape**
- ☐ **4 pieces of string, cut into 12-inch lengths**
- ☐ **4 blank white index cards**
- ☐ **Pen**

- ☐ **Cotton swab**
- ☐ **Petroleum jelly**
- ☐ **Zippered sandwich bag**
- ☐ **Magnifying glass**

THE STEPS:

1. Tape a piece of string to each of the index cards. The string will be used to hang the cards in different locations.

2. Label the four cards: "Control," "Indoors," "Yard," and "Tree."

3. Dip the cotton swab into the petroleum jelly. Use it to coat most of the surface of one side of each card with a thin layer of petroleum jelly.

4. Hang the "Indoors" card somewhere inside your house. Hang the "Yard" card in your yard (or any open grassy area) and the "Tree" card under the branches of a tree. Be sure to hang the cards in locations where they will be undisturbed for three days. Place the "Control" card inside the zippered sandwich bag.

5. After three days, go to each of your sampling locations and get your index cards. Use the magnifying glass to examine each card for aerosols that were caught in the petroleum jelly. Compare the cards to the "Control" card. Record your findings in the data table below.

Observations: Which card collected the most aerosols? What aerosols do you think were trapped in the petroleum jelly? What do you think are the sources of the particles you collected?

The Hows and Whys: Aerosols are any tiny particles that become airborne in the wind. Some examples are dust, smoke, car exhaust or other pollution, pollen, and ash from volcanoes. Aerosols are more concentrated in the air near where they were formed; for example, you'd find more ash particles in the air near a volcano and fewer particles the farther away you travel.

KICK IT UP A NOTCH: **Think of a few other locations where you might be able to sample. Could you collect a sample near a busy road? Or perhaps in different rooms of your house? How do you think those samples would differ?**

	CONTROL	INDOORS	YARD	TREE
PARTICLE COUNT: (NONE/LOW/ MEDIUM/HIGH)				

CHAPTER 3

CLOUDS

Cloud watching is one of the most basic ways that people can interpret the weather. For example, a puffy white cloud on a summer day can be a beautiful sight, while a dark gray thundercloud could send you running indoors.

Generally, clouds form when warm, moist air rises up, then cools in the colder and higher parts of the atmosphere. **Water vapor** is the gas form of water, but as it cools, the water vapor condenses—or turns into droplets of liquid water—in the air. These collections of suspended water droplets are clouds. In some climates and seasons, clouds can also be made up of ice crystals suspended in the sky.

Clouds can form almost anywhere on Earth and in any climate, so long as there is warm, moist air available. However, in extremely dry regions, such as deserts, clouds are scarce.

Here are some of the most common cloud types and what they might tell us to expect in the weather forecast.

High Clouds (16,000 to 43,000 ft)

Cirrocumulus Clouds

Cirrocumulus

Cirrocumulus clouds look like long rows of tiny cotton balls all lined up together high in the sky. They usually mean that you can expect fair weather. If you live near the tropics, though they might be a sign that a hurricane is on the way!

Cirrus

These wispy clouds form high in the atmosphere—about three to seven miles above Earth's surface. A few cirrus clouds can be a sign that fair weather is here to stay for a while. But if there is a web of cirrus clouds in the sky, a warm front might be on its way, signaling a change in the weather.

Cirrostratus

These are sheetlike clouds made of ice crystals that can spread out over the entire sky. They are so thin that you can often see the Sun or Moon through them. In the daytime, they make the sunshine look milky. When you see cirrostratus clouds, it usually means a storm is coming soon.

Mid-Level Clouds (7,000 to 23,000 ft)

Altocumulus Clouds

Altocumulus

Fluffy gray and white altocumulus clouds form in groups in the atmosphere below where you find cirrus clouds. If you see them in the morning when you wake up, and it's warm and humid, you may see a thunderstorm in the afternoon.

Altostratus

These blue-gray clouds cover the whole sky, making the Sun or Moon appear a bit fuzzy. They mean that a storm with lots of continuous rain or snow could be on its way.

Low Clouds (surface to 7,000 ft, though some can grow taller)

Stratus

Stratus clouds make the sky appear gray and misty. They look like a fog that hasn't quite reached Earth's surface. If you see them, grab your umbrella: Drizzly weather usually accompanies these gray skies.

Nimbostratus

Gray, rough, gloomy nimbostratus clouds are located close to the ground. They sometimes cover the whole sky and almost always mean that rain or snow is on the way.

Cumulonimbus

These clouds are enormous! They are puffy and gray and white, like cumulus clouds, but can grow miles into the atmosphere. Cumulonimbus clouds are usually bad news: They can bring rain, hail, lightning, or even tornadoes.

Cumulonimbus Cloud

Cumulus

These puffy, cottony clouds are what you think of when you imagine a cloud. They are gray and white and usually have a flat bottom. They don't give you a lot of hints about the weather; you can see them both in fair weather and before storms. But if the top of the clouds looks like a head of cauliflower, that could mean rain showers are coming.

Unusual Clouds (not classified by height)

Lenticular Clouds

Lenticular

Lenticular clouds are formed when moving air hits a barrier such as a mountain range. These clouds don't tell us much about the weather, but they look really cool.

How Does It Do That?

Clouds look like puffy cotton balls, but, amazingly, they're just made of air and water. How do they get up there in the sky? Evaporation!

1. **Water in clouds begins on Earth.** As water in oceans, lakes, and rivers is warmed by the Sun and blown in the wind, it begins to evaporate. **Evaporation** is the process by which a liquid turns into a gas: In this case, liquid water turns into the gas form of water—called water vapor.

2. **Warm water rises.** Air high in the atmosphere is colder than air closer to Earth's surface. When water vapor in the air is warmed by the Sun, it rises up to this colder part of the atmosphere. Cool air causes the water vapor to condense, turning it into liquid water droplets or ice crystals.

3. **Water droplets form a cloud.** To make a cloud, you need many, many water droplets. **Condensation** happens more easily and quickly if the water vapor has a solid object to condense upon. Consider water dripping down the outside of a cold soda can on a hot summer day. There is water vapor in the humid air, but you can't see it until it encounters the soda can surface and appears as drops of water. Just like on a soda can, water vapor can condense or freeze on particles of dust and

THE WATER CYCLE

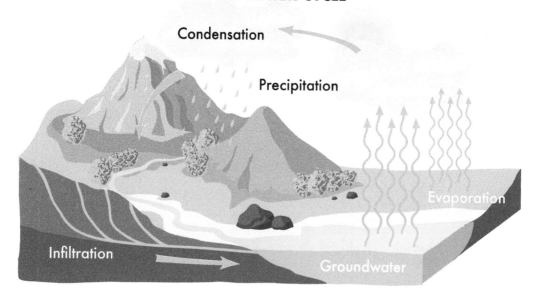

pollen in the atmosphere, creating tiny water droplets or ice crystals. When enough droplets or crystals form, you have a cloud!

4. **Clouds can result from a region's geography.** Lenticular and stratus clouds form when wind blows into the side of a mountain or hill and pushes the air high up into the atmosphere. As this cool air rises, clouds form.

5. **Clouds also form when masses of air meet each other at Earth's surface.** These large masses of air are called fronts. Mid-level clouds, high clouds, and rain clouds can all form at **warm fronts**, where a warm mass of air slides on top of a cold air mass.

6. **A cold front** occurs when a mass of cold air slides underneath a mass of warm air, thrusting the warm air higher into the atmosphere. Cumulus and other rain clouds often form this way.

7. **Clouds provide shade from the Sun.** Clouds act like an umbrella in the sky, blocking the Sun's rays and reflecting them back into space. A cloudy area will be darker and cooler than it would be on a sunny day.

TO THE EXTREMES!

Could you live somewhere that has an average of only two hours of sunlight a day? That's what it's like in Tórshavn, Faroe Islands—the cloudiest place on Earth. The Faroe Islands, which are part of Denmark, are located about halfway between Norway and Iceland. Tórshavn, the capital city, is likely so cloudy because it is bordered by two mountains. If warm, moist air rises in the atmosphere but it doesn't rise high enough to pass over a mountain, the air can get trapped, resulting in clouds and rain.

The least cloudy place on Earth is the Atacama Desert in western South America. It has almost no clouds and hardly any rain at all. These cloud-free skies make the Atacama Desert a popular place for stargazing, and it's home to some of the world's most powerful telescopes. With no clouds in the way, nighttime in the Atacama offers spectacular views of the Milky Way, too.

Get Involved!

In the experiments in this chapter, you'll make clouds, learn how clouds affect temperature, and even try to forecast your local weather based on the clouds! During these experiments, remember the concepts we learned in this chapter, including condensation and cloud formation.

EXPERIMENTS

Clouds in the Kitchen

QUICK QUERY

The Big Idea: In nature, clouds form when water droplets meet colder layers of the atmosphere high in the sky. But did you know that you can also make a cloud in a jar in your kitchen? In this experiment, you'll put boiling water and aerosol particles in the jar.

 Cautions: Have an adult lab partner help you with boiling the water. Be careful with the boiling water so that you don't get burned, and remember to handle glass jars very gently so they don't break. Be careful with the food coloring if you use it, as it can stain clothing and carpets.

MATERIALS:

- ☐ **1 cup boiling water**
- ☐ **1-pint glass jar with metal lid**
- ☐ **Food coloring (optional)**
- ☐ **Spoon (if you use food coloring)**
- ☐ **Hair spray**
- ☐ **Ice cubes**

THE STEPS:

1. Have an adult help you pour 1 cup of boiling water into the 1-pint glass jar. If you're using food coloring, quickly add it to the water, and immediately stir it in with a spoon.

2. Quickly spray the hair spray into the jar and put the lid on top.

3. Put ice cubes on top of the metal lid of the jar.

4. Watch the air in the jar above the water and observe what happens.

Observations: What happened after you added ice to the lid of the jar? Is it what you expected to happen?

The Hows and Whys: In nature, warm, moist air rises up and cools as it gets to the higher, colder parts of the atmosphere. That's exactly what is happening in this experiment, too! The hair spray particles floating around in the jar act just like the dust and pollen particles in our atmosphere. The warm, moist air in the jar rises up, is cooled by the cold air created by the ice, and then condenses on the particles of hair spray—creating your very own cloud!

KICK IT UP A NOTCH: Try doing the same experiment with jars of different sizes or with different amounts of boiling water inside the jars. How do you think the size of the jar and the amount of water will change what happens?

- -

Staying Cool Under a Cloud

OBSERVATION DECK

The Big Idea: Clouds block heat from the Sun, so it's cooler on a cloudy day than on a sunny day. But how much cooler? In this experiment, you'll create sunny and cloudy days indoors, tracking just how much relief from the heat clouds can provide.

Cautions: Ask an adult lab partner to help you with cutting the bottles and plugging the lamp into the wall. After the experiment is over, let the lamp cool down for at least 15 minutes before handling it. For best results, the heat bulb should be 60 to 75 watts, but be sure to choose a bulb and wattage that follows the lamp manufacturer's guidelines.

MATERIALS:

- [ ] **Desk-style lamp with heat bulb**
- [ ] **2 clean, empty 2-liter plastic bottles with caps on**
- [ ] **Scissors**
- [ ] **2 pieces of black construction paper**
- [ ] **Tape**
- [ ] **Cloud shapes cut out of aluminum foil**
- [ ] **2 indoor or outdoor thermometers, for measuring air temperature**
- [ ] **Pen or pencil**
- [ ] **Stopwatch**

1. Put the heat lamp on a table near an electrical outlet. Do not turn the lamp on yet.

2. Take any labels off the plastic bottles, then use the scissors to cut them about one-third of the way down from the top. You'll use only the bottle tops in this experiment, so dispose of the rest of the plastic.

3. Cut the black construction paper into two circles just a little bigger around than the bottoms of the cut pieces of the bottles.

4. Tape the foil clouds to the front of one of the bottles.

5. Place the bottles side by side on the table, 6 to 8 inches in front of the heat-lamp bulb. Both bottles should be the same distance from the lamp, and the bulb should shine into the front of each bottle, not the top. Each bottle should get the same amount of heat. The cut-out clouds covering the front of one of the bottles should face the lamp, blocking some of the lamp's heat.

6. Place a black construction paper circle under each bottle, with a thermometer lying on top of the circle. You should be able to read the temperature through the back of each bottle.

7. Record the starting temperature of each bottle in the data table on the next page at "0 minutes."

8. Start the stopwatch and turn on the lamp at the same time. Check the temperature every minute, and record that number in the data table. Do this every minute for 10 minutes.

Observations: Did the two bottles have different temperatures? If so, which one was warmer, and which one was cooler?

The Hows and Whys: During the daytime, clouds in our atmosphere reflect some of the Sun's light and heat back into space, helping us stay cool. In this experiment, the aluminum foil clouds serve the same function. Because the foil clouds reflect the light and heat away from the bottle, they keep the environment cooler.

continued >

KICK IT UP A NOTCH: Do the experiment again, but this time, try attaching clouds with different shapes to the cloud bottle. Observe whether this change makes any difference in the temperature. You can also try placing the clouds in different locations on the bottle. Do higher clouds block more light and heat than lower ones?

	CLOUD BOTTLE TEMPERATURE	CLEAR BOTTLE TEMPERATURE
0 MINUTES		
1 MINUTE		
2 MINUTES		
3 MINUTES		
4 MINUTES		
5 MINUTES		
6 MINUTES		
7 MINUTES		
8 MINUTES		
9 MINUTES		
10 MINUTES		

Cloud Journaling

TAKE IT OUTSIDE

The Big Idea: Can you predict the weather by reading the clouds? Find out by keeping a cloud journal for a week! Twice each day, you'll go outside, look up at the sky, and record the types of clouds you see, as well as the temperature outside. The information I've provided about the different kinds of clouds will help you make a prediction about what kind of weather could be on the way. Will the cloud and temperature information help you make accurate predictions?

 Cautions: None! This activity is safe for all ages.

MATERIALS:

- ☐ **Cloud type descriptions from pages 22 to 25**
- ☐ **Outdoor thermometer**
- ☐ **Notebook (or use the data table on page 35)**
- ☐ **Pen or pencil**

continued >

THE STEPS:

1. Pick a time in the morning and a time in the afternoon when you're able to observe and record the clouds. When the time comes, grab your cloud type descriptions, outdoor thermometer, notebook, and pen or pencil and then head outside.

2. In your notebook, write down the date and time. Use the thermometer to take an outdoor temperature reading, and record that in your notebook as well.

3. Next, find a comfy spot where you can sit down on the ground and look up at the sky. Use the cloud type descriptions to identify the clouds that you see, and record the cloud types in your notebook. Make any other notes you think will be helpful, such as the size or color of the clouds. Underneath your observations, write a weather prediction based on the clouds you saw. Rain? Snow? Clear skies?

4. Record the date, time, temperature, cloud types, and predictions twice a day for three to five days in your notebook or in the data table on the next page.

5. Each day, look back at the previous day's prediction. Put a check mark next to the prediction if it was correct and an *X* if it was wrong.

Observations: What kinds of clouds were the most common? Do you notice any relationship between the clouds you saw and the temperatures you recorded? Were you able to successfully predict any weather phenomena by looking at the clouds?

The Hows and Whys: Clouds tell us about the conditions in our atmosphere and what those conditions can mean for the weather ahead. Meteorologists look at clouds from the ground, from airplanes, and from orbiting satellites to help make their weather forecasts.

KICK IT UP A NOTCH: **Use the barometer you made in chapter 2 (page 15) to record atmospheric pressure during each sampling period in addition to temperature and cloud types. See if you notice any relationships among air pressure, temperature, and cloud types.**

DATE AND TIME	OUTDOOR TEMPERATURE	CLOUDS OBSERVED	WEATHER PREDICTION
DAY 1 MORNING			
DAY 1 AFTERNOON			
DAY 2 MORNING			
DAY 2 AFTERNOON			
DAY 3 MORNING			
DAY 3 AFTERNOON			
DAY 4 MORNING			
DAY 4 AFTERNOON			
DAY 5 MORNING			
DAY 5 AFTERNOON			

CHAPTER 4

RAIN

Sprinkle. Spritz. Drizzle. Downpour. These are all names that we've given to the water that falls out of our sky—rain. Fresh water is necessary for life on Earth, and **precipitation**, such as rain, is one way we get it.

It can rain in almost any climate, all over the world. In order for rain to form, there needs to be moisture in the air and a temperature above freezing. That means that rain is very rare in dry climates, such as deserts, and cold climates, such as the Arctic and Antarctic.

How Does It Do That?

Rain obviously falls from the sky, but how did it get up there in the first place? And what made those drops eventually fall to the ground?

1. **It all starts with the Sun.** The Sun's heat warms water in oceans, lakes, rivers, streams, and the soil. Some of that water evaporates, becoming water vapor in the air. Plants also release water vapor into the air. You've probably heard people talking about the amount of water vapor in the air by using the term **humidity**. On a humid day, there is a lot of water vapor in the air.

2. **Air currents take the water vapor higher into the atmosphere, where it is cooler.** The lower temperatures cause the water vapor to condense onto dust and other particles to form water droplets. These water droplets form clouds.

3. **Water droplets in clouds combine to form bigger droplets.** When they become too big and heavy to float in the air, these water droplets fall to the ground as precipitation—rain, snow, sleet, or hail. As rain falls from clouds, most of it falls into the ocean or soil. People, animals, and plants all get the water they need to live from the soil or from bodies of water. That water eventually ends up back in the soil, ocean, or other bodies of water, and the process begins all over again.

4. **The amount of water on Earth doesn't change much.** We can reuse Earth's water over and over again. And that's exactly what we do because of the **water cycle**. (See the diagram on page 27.) The water cycle doesn't really have a beginning or end. Rather, it represents how water in (for example) the ocean becomes water in a cloud, which turns into water we can drink, which eventually ends up back in the ocean.

5. **Wind is an important part of the water cycle.** If there was no wind, water vapor would go straight up into the atmosphere, get cold, and come straight back down as rain. But instead air currents blow the clouds around in our atmosphere. This moves water droplets from place to place and keeps them suspended in the air for longer than they would be without wind.

6. **Too much of a good thing.** Although rain is usually good news for people, plants, and animals, too much can be dangerous. For example, when a thunderstorm brings heavy rain, sometimes there is a **flash flood**. In a flash flood, rain comes quickly and water rises so fast that homes and roads can flood.

DROUGHTS

When a region gets a lot less rain than it normally would over a long period of time, we call it a **drought**. But "less rain than it normally would" can mean a lot of different things, depending on people's different situations.

A long stretch with no rain can cause soil to dry out and plants and animals to die. It can cause streams and rivers to shrink or even dry up. Usually, rain fills lakes, ponds, and reservoirs with water that people can use in dry times. However, after too much time with little or no rain, this water either gets used up or evaporates. That's when water supply problems begin, and that's often the beginning of a drought.

The average American uses 80 to 100 gallons of water a day—for drinking, cooking, bathing, washing hands, and even flushing the toilet. That comes to more than 30,000 gallons every year. That's a lot of water!

We can use less water by following a few simple tips. For example, try to use water more than once. Did you give your dog a bath this weekend? Think about using eco-friendly pet shampoos so that you can use Sparky's bathwater to water the plants! Do you have a big backyard? Think about replacing that water-guzzling grass with some native plants that are less thirsty.

TO THE EXTREMES!

What's the wettest place on Earth? It is the village of Mawsynram in northeast India. On average, Mawsynram gets about a whopping 39 feet of rain each year. And most of that rain—90 percent of it—falls between May and October. This period is called monsoon season. (The word *monsoon* comes from an Arabic word meaning "season.")

A **monsoon** happens when the Sun heats the ocean and the land unevenly in certain regions. In the summer, the land is usually warmer than the ocean. So all season long, moist air from the ocean blows onto the land and rises up in the atmosphere. For nearly six straight months, this phenomenon causes almost constant clouds, high winds, and heavy rain.

What's the driest place on Earth? Well, you already learned about this region in chapter 3: the Atacama Desert! Arica, Chile, in the Atacama Desert holds the world record for the longest recorded dry period. The city receives an average of only 0.03 inches of rain each year. In fact, Arica once had no rain at all for over 14 straight years!

As the global climate changes, deserts are changing, too. Some deserts are getting hotter, while others are actually getting wetter. Either way, the animals and plants that live in these environments are having to learn to either adapt or leave to survive. Not all of them will succeed.

Get Involved!

In the following experiments, you'll dig into how rain works and how it affects our environment. You'll learn how rain interacts with different types of soil, how the water cycle works, and how to figure out the amount of rain that fell during a storm. Let's get started!

Soil Soaker

QUICK QUERY

The Big Idea: Have you ever wondered what causes a flood? Well, it's more than just a lot of rain! In this experiment, you'll test different types of soil to see which ones hold water and which ones let the water pass right on through. What soil material do you think will hold on to the most water?

> **Cautions:** None! This activity should be safe for all ages.

MATERIALS:

- ☐ **Coffee filters**
- ☐ **Funnel**
- ☐ **Glass or plastic jar**
- ☐ **Pea gravel**
- ☐ **Liquid measuring cup**
- ☐ **Water**
- ☐ **Timer**
- ☐ **Pen or pencil**
- ☐ **Sand**
- ☐ **Potting soil**
- ☐ **Powdered clay**

continued >

THE STEPS:

1. Put the coffee filter in the funnel, then place the funnel on top of the glass or plastic jar. The spout should point down into the jar.

2. Fill the coffee filter about two-thirds of the way up with pea gravel.

3. Use your measuring cup to measure 50 mL of water.

4. Set your timer for 2 minutes, but don't start it yet.

5. Pour the water over the pea gravel and immediately start your 2-minute timer.

6. At the end of the time, pour the water that has filtered into the jar back into your measuring cup. Record how much water got through.

7. Take the filter with the wet pea gravel out of the funnel. Replace it with a clean coffee filter, and fill the new filter two-thirds of the way up with sand, potting soil, or powdered clay.

8. Repeat the steps of the experiment until you have tested every material in the same manner. Always remember to record your results in the data table that follows—in this case, how much water filtered through each material.

Observations: Which substance held the most water? Why do you think that is?

The Hows and Whys: Large particles—such as pea gravel—don't pack together as tightly as smaller particles. Water can filter through the spaces between the rocks and into the jar below. The same thing happens in nature. When rain falls on a rocky area of ground, the water can filter down through the rocks. But tightly packed clay soil may be more prone to flooding.

KICK IT UP A NOTCH: Try doing this experiment again with other materials. What is the soil in your neighborhood made up of? Try a scoop from your backyard in this experiment, and compare the amount of water to your earlier results. Is your soil more similar to sand or clay?

MATERIAL	VOLUME OF FILTERED WATER
PEA GRAVEL	
SAND	
POTTING SOIL	
POWDERED CLAY	

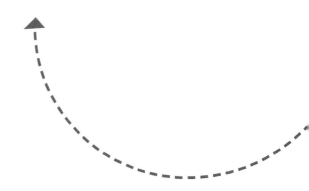

Water Cycle in a Bag

OBSERVATION DECK

The Big Idea: The water cycle is essential to life on Earth. In this experiment, you'll create your own tiny model of Earth, with a plastic sandwich bag acting as a stand-in for Earth's atmosphere. What do you think will happen when heat from the Sun reaches the water inside your bag?

 Cautions: This activity should be safe for all ages. But be careful with the food coloring if you use it, as it can stain clothing and carpets.

MATERIALS:

- ☐ **Liquid measuring cup**
- ☐ **Water**
- ☐ **Blue food coloring (optional)**
- ☐ **Zippered sandwich bag**
- ☐ **Permanent marker**
- ☐ **Tape**

THE STEPS:

1. Measure out ¼ cup of water. If you are using blue food coloring, add it now. Set the water aside.

2. Use the marker to draw waves near the bottom of the zippered bag. Then draw a cloud and a sun near the top of the bag.

3. Open the bag and pour the water inside. Zip the bag closed. Make sure it's completely sealed.

4. Tape the bag filled with water to a window. Be sure to choose a window that will get sunlight.

5. Check on the bag each day for a few days until you notice changes. Be sure to record the changes you see.

Observations: What changes did you notice in the bag after a few days of heat from the Sun?

The Hows and Whys: In the experiment, the sandwich bag acts like Earth's atmosphere, trapping the Sun's heat and Earth's moisture. The water at the bottom of the bag acts like the ocean, and as it heats, it turns into water vapor. At the top of the bag, the water vapor condenses into liquid droplets—a cloud.

KICK IT UP A NOTCH: Make several water cycles in bags. Tape one to each window in your house and see which window gives the best results.

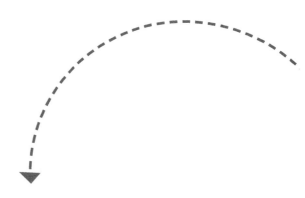

Rain Tracker

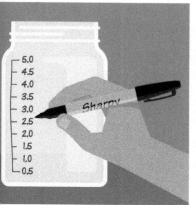

TAKE IT OUTSIDE

The Big Idea: In this experiment, you will build your own rain gauge—a tool used to collect and measure rain. You'll place it outside during a rainstorm, collecting the gauge after the storm to see how much rain fell. Build several gauges to test the rainfall in different spots—for example, under a tree or in a place where rain rolls off the roof of a house. Did the amount of rain in your gauges match your predictions?

 Cautions: Handle glass jars carefully so that they don't break.

MATERIALS:

- ☐ **Glass jars**
- ☐ **Funnels**
- ☐ **Permanent marker**
- ☐ **Ruler**
- ☐ **Duct tape**
- ☐ **Pen or pencil**

THE STEPS:

1. Decide how many locations you'll need rain gauges for. Be sure to have that many jars and funnels.

2. Use a permanent marker and a ruler to mark and label the side of each jar every half inch for 5 inches. You'll do this by lining up the bottom of the ruler next to the bottom of the jar, then drawing a small line every half inch. Label the lines "0.5 in," "1 in," "1.5 in," "2 in," and so on, up to "5 in."

3. Place a funnel in the top of every jar. Use the duct tape to fasten each funnel securely to its jar. You don't want the rain to knock it off!

4. Now place your rain gauges in a variety of locations and wait for the rain to fall.

5. After it rains, collect your rain gauges and record how much rain is in each jar in the data table below using the measurement markings on the sides of the jars.

Observations: How much rain did each gauge collect? Was it more or less than you were expecting? Did the location of the rain gauge make any difference?

The Hows and Whys: A rain gauge is an important tool in a meteorologist's toolbox. Tracking how much rain falls every year for many years also gives us information about an area's climate—and if it is changing to become, on average, wetter or drier.

> KICK IT UP A NOTCH: Compare your findings with the local weather report. If your results differed from the official record of the amount of rain for the day, try to figure out why.

continued >

Rain Tracker *continued*

RAIN GAUGE LOCATION	RAINFALL MEASUREMENT

CHAPTER 5

SNOW

You might think that only very cold places have snow. That's partly true. To get snowy weather, a climate needs to have both moisture in the air and low temperatures. That's why hot, dry deserts don't get snow very often.

However, the temperature on the ground doesn't have much to do with snow formation. Snow forms high up in the atmosphere when the temperature there is below freezing—less than 32°F (0°C). After snowflakes form, they fall toward the ground. And if the temperature on the ground isn't too much warmer than freezing, you could be in for a snow day—woo-hoo!

How Does It Do That?

Just like rain, snow forms when warm, moist air rises into the atmosphere and forms a cloud. But what causes the cloud to form snow instead of rain?

1. **Water vapor freezes.** When snow forms, warm, moist air rises up into very cold air that is near or below the freezing temperature. The water vapor freezes into ice crystals instead of turning into water droplets.

2. **Ice crystals become snow.** As ice crystals drift down, they travel through rising warmer, moist air. If the moist air is slightly warmer than freezing, it will melt the edges of the crystals. These melted edges cause the crystals to stick together and become snowflakes. When enough crystals stick together, they become too heavy to float and fall to the ground as snow.

3. **Wet snow is the best snow for fun.** Snowflakes created in an environment with lots of warm, moist air are wet and sticky. This produces the biggest snowflakes. This kind of snow, called wet snow, is the best material for building a snowman or a snow fort.

4. **Skiers love "fresh powder."** Another type of snow, called dry snow, forms when smaller snowflakes fall through cold, dry air. The edges of the snowflakes never get a chance to melt, so they don't stick together. This type of dry, powdery snow is ideal for skiers.

Strike a Pose

Individual snowflakes can be beautiful, but millions of snowflakes together can make beautiful formations, too! Here are some snow art shows brought to you by nature:

Glaciers

Glaciers are made up of snow that has piled up over many years. Each layer of snow is pressed down by the weight of the snow that falls on top of it. The snow is pressed down so much that eventually it becomes ice—a glacier.

Glaciers

As the snow is compressed, the structure of the ice changes. These changes cause the compressed ice to scatter and reflect blue light, causing some glaciers to appear blue.

As Earth's climate changes, many glaciers around the world are shrinking.

Snow Cornice

Snow Cornice

A **snow cornice** forms when snow is blown by the wind at the sharp edge of a ridge or cliff face. The wind creates a ledge of snow and ice that overhangs the top of the cliff.

Be careful if you see a snow cornice! The ledge of snow it creates can fall off the cliff's edge. This is a risk for **avalanches**, masses of snow that slide down mountains.

Snow Penitentes

Snow penitentes are spikes of snow that are compacted by certain patterns of melting and evaporation. They form most commonly in mountains, especially in the Andes Mountains along the west coast of South America. The pointy tops of penitentes point toward the location of the noon sun, and they usually form in rows going east to west.

TO THE EXTREMES!

Imagine you're riding a bus, and as you look out the window, all you see is white snow. Above you, below you, beside you—snow is everywhere. Well, that's what life is like in the mountains of the Japanese Alps on the island of Honshu. This area has the deepest snow in the world—or, at least, in the parts of the world where people live.

A highway that goes through a snowy canyon in these mountains has walls of snow as high as 66 feet, which is as tall as a seven-story building! If you ride in a bus or car on this road in the middle of winter, it will feel like you are driving through a never-ending tunnel of snow.

Is there a place where it never snows? Absolutely! It has never snowed in the very warm climates of Guam, in the Pacific Ocean, and the US Virgin Islands, in the Caribbean Sea. Both islands have high temperatures year-round. The coolest they get is about 50°F (10°C), so it's never cold enough for snow to form.

Get Involved!

Now that you've learned how snow forms in the atmosphere and how it ends up down on the ground, let's see some of this science in action!

EXPERIMENTS

Frost in a Can

QUICK QUERY

The Big Idea: Have you ever noticed frost on a car windshield on a cold morning? Frost forms at low temperatures when condensation—water vapor that becomes liquid water on a surface—freezes instead of remaining liquid. In this experiment, you will create your own frost by using cans, ice, and salt.

 Cautions: Be careful of any sharp edges on the opening of the metal cans.

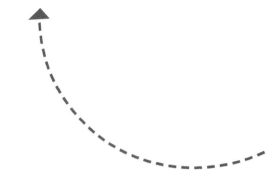

MATERIALS:

- ☐ **Crushed ice**
- ☐ **2 empty, clean metal cans (like those from canned soup)**
- ☐ **Salt**

THE STEPS:

1. Add crushed ice to both metal cans.

2. Sprinkle salt on top of the ice in one can. The other can should have just ice inside.

3. Wait about 5 minutes.

4. Check the cans again. You should notice that frost has formed on the outside of one of the cans.

Observations: Why do you think the frost formed on the outside of that can? What do you think the purpose of the salt was?

The Hows and Whys: Have you ever seen someone pouring salt on sidewalks or roads after it snows? This is done because salt lowers the melting point of ice. So when you add salt to an icy sidewalk, the ice will melt even if the temperature outside is still below freezing. This helps prevent slippery roads and sidewalks. We used the same property of salt here!

KICK IT UP A NOTCH: Try doing this experiment again by sprinkling other substances on top of the ice. Would sugar or baking soda have the same effect as salt? Why or why not?

How Much Water Is in Snow?

 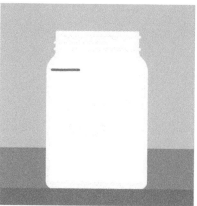 

TAKE IT OUTSIDE

The Big Idea: Fallen snow is made of snowflakes and air—but exactly how much water is in snow? In this experiment, you'll get to see how much water is in a few inches of snow. How much water do you think will result when the snow melts?

> ⚠ **Cautions:** Handle glass jars carefully so that they don't break.

MATERIALS:

- ☐ **Glass jar**
- ☐ **Snow**
- ☐ **Dry-erase marker**
- ☐ **Ruler**
- ☐ **Pen or pencil**

THE STEPS:

1. Bring your glass jar outside on a snowy day. Fill the jar almost to the top with snow. Use the dry-erase marker to mark the level of the snow on the side of the jar. Measure the height of the snow with the ruler and record this number in the data table on the next page.

2. Bring the jar inside, then wait until all of the snow has melted.

3. After the snow has melted, use your dry-erase marker to mark the level of water in the jar. Use a ruler to measure the height of the water, and record the value in the data table.

4. Divide the number of inches of snow you started with by the number of inches of water you ended up with. That's how much snow it took to make 1 inch of water.

Observations: Did the melted snow produce more or less water than you were expecting?

The Hows and Whys: When snowflakes fall, they don't pack together tightly, so there is a lot of air between them. For this reason, snow carries much less water than rain. Though a storm bringing 12 inches of rain could result in a flood, a storm bringing 12 inches of snow won't be nearly as wet—even after the snow melts.

KICK IT UP A NOTCH: Do this experiment several times over the course of the winter, and record your findings each time. Do some types of snow contain more water than others?

INCHES OF SNOW	INCHES OF WATER	SNOW PER 1 INCH OF WATER (INCHES SNOW/INCHES WATER)

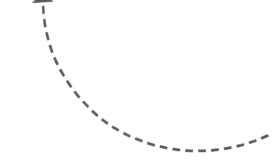

CHAPTER 6

FOG

You get up in the morning and look out your window . . . and you see almost nothing. The tree in your neighbor's yard isn't visible, and you can't see the mailbox at the curb. Are you still asleep? Nope! It's just a foggy morning!

Fog basically forms like a cloud that touches the ground. And as you might expect, walking or driving through this cloud can be tricky. When fog is dense, visibility—how far a person can see—is very low. That means that driving a car or travel of any kind can be dangerous. Have you ever had to travel in fog?

In general, fog can form in most places with moisture in the air and temperature differences between the atmosphere and Earth's surface.

TO THE EXTREMES!

In most climates, we take for granted the fact that on a typical day, we can hop in a car or bus and get from point A to point B. A foggy day is only an occasional inconvenience. But that's not the case in the Grand Banks, just southeast of the island of Newfoundland in Canada.

With about 200 foggy days per year, the Grand Banks is one of the foggiest places in the whole world. Why is it so foggy? This region is where a cold ocean current from the north and a warm ocean current from the south meet. The mixture of these two currents causes a regular fog to form over the whole area.

If a constant layer of fog isn't your thing, you could always move to the desert in the Southwest region of the United States. This area—covering parts of Nevada, Utah, Arizona, and New Mexico—has only a few days of dense fog in an average year.

How Does It Do That?

Just like there are different types of clouds, there are different types of fog. Let's find out what they are!

1. **Radiation fog.** Fog looks like a cloud near the ground, and in fact that's almost exactly what it is. Clouds form when very humid air rises up into colder parts of the atmosphere, condensing and forming water droplets. However, fog forms like an upside-down cloud. During the day, heat from the Sun warms the ground. But at night the ground is cooler. As moist air approaches the cool ground, it begins to condense, forming water droplets—just like a cloud. This type of fog is called **radiation fog**.

2. **Advection fog.** This type of fog forms when warm air meets a cool surface. You may see **advection fog** along the West Coast of the United States. Cold ocean currents keep the air above the water colder than the air above the land.

3. **Valley fog.** In pictures of regions with lots of mountains, you'll often notice fog filling the valleys between them. This **valley fog** commonly forms at night and in the early morning. At night, the cool ground high in the mountains causes fog to form. But this dense, foggy air is heavy, so it slowly slides down the slope of the mountains and into the valleys below.

4. **Steam fog.** This type of fog forms over the tops of lakes, usually in the fall and winter. How? If a mass of cold air is on top of a mass of warm air near a lake's surface, this can lead to the rising warm air pushing the cold air upward. As the warm air lifts the cool air, the two air masses mix. This cools down the moist air right above the lake's surface, causing **steam fog** to form. This fog can look like vertical wisps rising from a lake.

5. **Ice fog.** If the temperature becomes colder than 14°F (−10°C), **ice fog** can form. Instead of water vapor turning into water droplets, extremely cold air temperatures can turn water vapor directly into small ice crystals. This type of fog is most common in cold places such as Alaska and the North and South Poles.

TRICK OR TREAT

Fog is probably the top weather phenomenon used in horror movies. Monsters lurk in the fog in dozens of movies, and you may have even seen a fog machine or two while trick-or-treating in your neighborhood. Why is fog so creepy? Dense fog makes it really difficult to see. So adding fog to a movie makes it easy for the film to hide scary villains . . . until they pop out suddenly.

In real life, fog probably isn't hiding a monster or a creepy dude with a chain saw. However, fog can still be dangerous for other reasons. For example, in dense fog you might not be able to see well enough to drive safely or to find your way on foot.

What determines visibility in the fog? It has a lot to do with the amount of water vapor in the air and the size of the water droplets that form the fog (bigger droplets mean lower visibility). Also, in an area with lots of smoke and pollution in the air, fog can become very dense even without much water vapor.

Get Involved!

All right, let's grab our supplies and get ready to go into the fog! In the upcoming experiment, we'll try to figure out the best way to see through a foggy night.

Seeing Through the Fog

TAKE IT OUTSIDE

The Big Idea: Fog lamps are special lights on some cars that can be found below the regular headlights. How do fog lamps on a car work? Go out on a foggy day and test it out! In this experiment, you'll shine a flashlight up high, at waist level, and near the ground. What happens when the light hits the fog?

 Cautions: Have an adult lab partner go with you. Do not walk out onto a road, driveway, or parking lot when visibility is low. Be sure that you are standing somewhere you know is safe while you make your observations.

MATERIALS:

☐ **A foggy evening/morning**

☐ **Flashlight**

☐ **Pen or pencil**

THE STEPS:

1. Go outside on a foggy evening or morning when it is dark. Choose a safe location where you will be able to see some kind of markings on the ground.

2. Shine the flashlight directly in front of you. With the flashlight in this position, can you see anything in front of you? Can you see any markings on the ground? Would you say that visibility is good, okay, bad, or very bad?

3. Now crouch down near the ground and shine the flashlight straight in front of you. Answer the same questions you answered in step 2.

4. Next, stand all the way up and hold the flashlight above your head. Shine the light forward, but keep the light at the same level above your head. Again, answer the questions from step 2.

5. Go inside and record your results in the data table below.

Observations: Which flashlight position made it easiest to see markings on the ground? Which position made it easiest to see directly in front of you?

The Hows and Whys: Fog lamps on cars work differently from headlights. Fog lamps shine down onto the road so that drivers can see the road beneath the fog and stay safely in their own lanes. Cars are built with fog lamps because regular headlights often shine up and into the fog, which is bad for visibility. The light from the headlights reflects off the fog, making it difficult to see.

KICK IT UP A NOTCH: **Try this experiment again with several different types of lights. Try flashlights with incandescent bulbs and LED bulbs. Which provides the best visibility?**

- -

LEVEL OF FLASHLIGHT	LEVEL OF VISIBILITY
LOW	
MIDDLE	
HIGH	

CHAPTER 7

THUNDERSTORMS

Have you ever been outside on a hot summer afternoon when suddenly the sky starts to darken and strong gusts of wind begin to blow? The treetops sway forcefully with the breeze. In the distance, you see a bright flash light up the sky. Then moments later, you hear a loud *boom*! All of a sudden, heavy rain comes pouring down. It's time to get yourself inside to a safe place—a thunderstorm is on its way!

Thunderstorms are rain showers with thunder and lightning. They form inside cumulonimbus clouds. Gusty winds, heavy rain, hail—even tornadoes—all may happen during thunderstorms. A weaker thunderstorm is called a thundershower.

From the lightning bolts that streak across the sky to the loud rumbling sounds of thunder, a thunderstorm can be both exciting and frightening at the same time. But what causes the lightning and thunder that give us such a jolt? Let's read on to find out!

How Does It Do That?

Thunderstorms are pretty common. More than 45,000 of them occur around the world every day! But how much do you know about them? Let's read on to find out!

1. **Once again, it all starts with the Sun.** The Sun heats the ground, which warms the air above it. Thunderstorms form when this warm air rises and meets cold air high above in the sky.

2. **A thunderstorm needs movement.** The cooled air drops in the atmosphere, and then it warms up and rises again. This movement of cool air and warm air currents is called **convection**.

3. **It also needs lift.** The upward lift needed for the air to rise can be caused by fronts, sea breezes, or even mountains.

4. **And plenty of moisture.** As the warm air rises and meets the cooler air, water vapor condenses, and cumulus clouds take shape. Moisture is created in the form of drops of water. With enough movement and moisture, these cumulus clouds grow larger until they become cumulonimbus clouds. These gigantic clouds produce the large amounts of rainfall associated with thunderstorms.

5. **The stages of a storm:**

   • The first stage of a thunderstorm is the cumulus stage. A cumulus cloud is pushed up by an **updraft**, or a rising current of air. You may see a flash or two of lightning, but there is hardly any rain yet.

   • The second stage is the mature stage. As the updraft continues and rain starts to fall, a downward current of air forms called a **downdraft**. This downdraft along with the cooled air form a **gust front**, or gusty winds that stretch along the ground. During this stage, watch out for heavy rainfall, hail, strong winds, and lightning. Even tornadoes may occur!

   • The final stage of a thunderstorm is the dissipating stage. At this point, the updraft is weakened by the cooled air, the gust front starts to leave the storm, and there is less rainfall.

6. **There are different types of thunderstorms.** A single-cell thunder-storm is a short, weak storm, but it may produce brief heavy rain and lightning. A multicell storm is the most common thunderstorm in which multiple cells form along the gust front. Hail, flooding, or tornadoes may occur. **Supercell** storms are very strong storms that may last an hour or even longer. Most tornadoes form from supercells.

7. **Thunderstorms can happen anytime . . .** But they most often occur in the spring and summer months. You might notice, too, that they often happen in the afternoon or evening hours.

8. **. . . or anywhere.** While thunderstorms can occur anyplace on Earth, they happen most often in tropical regions. In the United States, the most thunderstorms happen in Florida, with more than 80 days of storms a year!

9. **Severe thunderstorms can cause a lot of damage.** Fires, power outages, and flooding are just a few of the things that make thunder-storms dangerous. A thunderstorm is considered severe when it has hail at least one inch or bigger or winds above 58 miles per hour.

Thunderstorm Clouds

Lightning Strikes

Lightning is the flash of light you see in the sky during a thunderstorm. It is a quick spark of electricity released into the atmosphere. When the negative charges, or electrons, in a cloud connect with the positive charges, or protons, on the ground below, lightning occurs.

Thunder is caused by lightning. Lightning quickly heats the air, causing it to grow or expand. This expansion produces the loud booming sound of thunder we hear. Light moves much faster than sound. That is why we see lightning first and then hear thunder.

Lightning can be extremely dangerous. It can start fires or cause power outages. It can cause serious injury—or even kill a person. If you see lightning and hear thunder soon after, head immediately indoors for safety. Don't use phones or cellphones or electronic equipment or take a shower. Water, metal, and electrical wires are all conductors of electricity.

Lightning

Hailstorm

HERE COMES THE HAIL!

Some thunderstorms produce hail, or small balls of ice, that fall from the sky. Hail is formed when drops of water are lifted high up into the atmosphere with the updraft of a storm until they freeze.

Thunderstorms with hail are called hailstorms. Most hail is about the size of a pea, but some can be much bigger. The biggest hail ever recorded was nearly eight inches in diameter! But even small hail can cause a lot of damage. Hail can leave dents in cars and cracks in windshields. It can damage homes, buildings, and even agricultural crops.

Get Involved!

Now that you know more about thunderstorms, are you ready to see what causes all those bright flashes, loud booms, and heavy rainfall? In the following experiments, you'll see how a thunderstorm is formed, what makes lightning light up the sky, and what causes the loud booms of thunder. Let's get started!

EXPERIMENTS

How Does a Storm Form?

  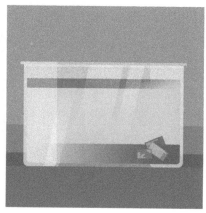

OBSERVATION DECK

The Big Idea: In general, storms form where masses of warm air meet masses of cool air in the atmosphere. In this experiment, you'll re-create this phenomenon using color-coded warm and cool water. What do you think will happen to the warm and cool water when they are combined in the clear plastic box?

 Cautions: Be careful with the food coloring, as it can stain clothing and carpets.

MATERIALS:

- ☐ **Water**
- ☐ **Cups**
- ☐ **Blue and red food coloring**
- ☐ **Spoon**
- ☐ **Ice-cube tray**
- ☐ **Clear plastic shoebox**

THE STEPS:

1. Pour some water into a cup and add a few drops of blue food coloring. Use the spoon to stir the mixture. Pour your blue water into the ice-cube tray and then place it in the freezer until it's frozen solid.

2. After the blue ice cubes have frozen, pour water that is barely warm into the clear plastic shoebox. Add a few drops of red food coloring to one side of the warm water in the box.

3. Add 3 or 4 blue ice cubes to the side of the box opposite to the red-colored water.

4. Observe what happens.

Observations: What happened as the blue ice cubes began to melt?

The Hows and Whys: In nature, thunderstorms can form when cold air masses meet warm air masses. The cold air masses sink down, pushing the warm air masses up. You can see the same thing happening in the experiment when the cold blue water pushes underneath the lukewarm red water. Where the red and blue water meet is where unstable air would appear in the atmosphere. This is the spot where thunderstorms form.

KICK IT UP A NOTCH: **Try a few different combinations of temperatures. For example, what happens if you use cold water in the shoebox instead of lukewarm water? What happens if you use hot water?**

- -

What Makes Lightning?

OBSERVATION DECK

The Big Idea: Lightning is an electrical charge produced during a thunder-storm. In this experiment, using a balloon, a light bulb, and your hair, you'll see just how electricity is created when two charges connect.

 Cautions: You may want to ask an adult with help blowing up the balloon. And remember: Hold the light bulb in your free hand. **It should not be in a lamp or light socket**.

MATERIALS:

☐ **Rubber balloon**

☐ **Light bulb**

THE STEPS:

1. Darken the room you're in by turning off lights and closing doors, blinds, and curtains.

2. Blow up the balloon to its full size.

3. Rub the balloon on your head for several seconds. Or ask a friend or sibling to rub it on their head.

4. Hold the balloon close to the end of the light bulb.

5. Observe what happens.

Observations: Why do you think the bulb lit up? What happened when you rubbed the balloon on your head?

The Hows and Whys: During a thunderstorm, clouds become charged with electricity. Electrical charges jump from one cloud to another, or from a cloud to the ground, causing lightning to strike. A similar thing is happening in this experiment. By rubbing the balloon on your hair, an electrical charge develops. When you hold the balloon close to the end of the light bulb, electrical charges connect, causing the bulb to light up.

KICK IT UP A NOTCH: Rub the balloon on your head for longer than you did the first time. Does it light up the bulb any faster or does it stay lit for a longer period of time? Or try this experiment with two balloons. Does the bulb light up faster or brighter?

What Makes Thunder?

 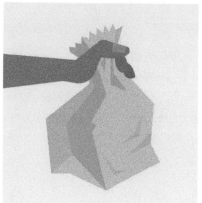 

QUICK QUERY

The Big Idea: You can't have thunder without lightning, but what is it that causes it to make that big booming sound? In this simple experiment, you'll use only two things—a paper bag and air—to create your own loud thunder.

> ⚠️ **Cautions:** None! This activity is safe for all ages.

MATERIALS:

 Brown paper lunch bag

THE STEPS:

1. Fill up the bag with air by blowing into it.

2. Twist the open end so that it is sealed. Hold it closed with your hand.

3. With your other hand, quickly hit the bag.

4. Observe what happens.

Observations: What happens to the air inside the bag when you hit it? What kind of sound did it make?

The Hows and Whys: As lightning strikes, the air heats up quickly, causing it to expand. This results in the loud booming sound we know as thunder. A similar thing is happening here. When you blow up the bag, you fill it with air. As you hit the bag, the air compresses and the bag breaks, causing the air to rush out. This moving air produces the loud sound you hear.

> **KICK IT UP A NOTCH:** Try this experiment with a larger paper bag, like a paper grocery bag. Is the sound louder?

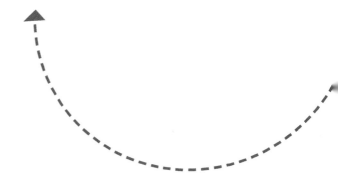

CHAPTER 8

DUST STORMS

When an area has dry soil and strong winds, it may experience dust storms. A **dust storm** happens when the winds are so strong that they pick up particles of soil, suspend them in the air for a while, and eventually drop the soil particles somewhere else.

Dust storms are most common in very dry places, such as the desert regions of northern Africa and the Arabian Peninsula. In the United States, they're most common in Southwestern states such as Arizona and New Mexico.

Have you ever experienced a dust storm in your home climate?

How Does It Do That?

1. **A dust storm usually starts with—you guessed it—a storm.** Thunderstorms can create very strong winds that pick up dust, sand, and soil from the dry ground. These dust storms can travel fast: 20 to 60 miles per hour. Once the particles are lifted off the ground, they rise higher and higher in the atmosphere in upward-moving air currents, called updrafts.

2. **Strong winds high in the atmosphere take the dust particles for a ride.** Depending on the size of the particles, they can stay suspended high in the atmosphere for anywhere from a few hours to 10 days or more. During this time, the dust can travel hundreds or thousands of miles away from where it was picked up. Eventually, the dust particles settle out of the atmosphere and fall to the ground.

3. **Traveling dust can have a big impact on our planet's ecosystems.** For example, scientists estimate that each year 20 million tons of dust are blown from the Sahara Desert in Africa all the way to the Amazon River basin in South America. This dust brings essential nutrients to the plants and animals of the Amazon Rainforest.

4. **Blowing dust can be hazardous.** Dust in the air is bad for human health. Very small dust particles—the ones small enough to be breathed in—can get stuck in your nose, mouth, and sinuses. These small particles can cause breathing and heart problems, including disorders such as pneumonia, asthma, and cardiovascular disease.

5. **Dust storms can impact Earth's weather patterns.** Clouds form more quickly and easily when particles called aerosols are in the atmosphere. These particles serve as a seed for water-droplet formation; water vapor encounters the particles and immediately begins to form droplets around them. Particles from dust storms are examples of aerosols and can have a major effect on local cloud formation.

6. **Human activities are having an impact on dust storms.** Forests and grasses have roots that keep soil in the ground. When people clear forests and grasslands for farms, houses, and other buildings, more soil is exposed, meaning it can be easily picked up into a dust storm. In addition, the warming climate makes soil dry out and plants die, exposing even more soil to the wind.

Dust storms can have a remarkable impact on landscapes. The photos here—from real dust storms—are both cool and devastating. Let's take a look at what dust storms look like from space, from the sky, and from the ground.

Dust storms carry so much dust and soil that they can even be seen from space! The first image, taken by a satellite orbiting Earth, shows winds carrying dust from the Sahara Desert 1,000 miles or more into the Atlantic Ocean.

The second photo, taken from a helicopter, shows a dust storm approaching and hitting Phoenix, Arizona. It moves in like a wall of dust, just ahead of a thunderstorm. The photographer and pilot were able to get to safety after taking this photo, but flying airplanes and helicopters in dust storms can be very dangerous.

This last photograph shows a building buried in sand after a dust storm and was taken in Oklahoma in 1936. At this time, America's southern prairie states were experiencing a drought. They were also hit with many dust storms that were so severe, they were often called "black blizzards." Because of the choking storms, people started referring to the region as the Dust Bowl. The impact of the Dust Bowl era damaged the area's ecosystem and farms for many years.

TO THE EXTREMES!

It may not be too surprising that the Sahara Desert is dusty. In fact, more than half of the dust that ends up in the ocean was lifted from the Sahara. A specific region of the southern Sahara called the Bodélé Depression is the dustiest place on Earth. It has dust storms carrying plumes of dust into the air more than 100 days per year.

Can people live in the dusty Sahara? Absolutely! About 2.5 million people live in the Sahara Desert. They either live permanently near sources of water, or they travel around from place to place to graze their herds of sheep, goats, or camels.

Although dust storms can happen in most climates, they are unlikely to occur in an area with lots of moisture and plants, like a forest or a rain forest.

Get Involved!

Dust storms can be dangerous to experience in real life, but we can learn about them by doing experiments at home. Here, we'll study how wind speed affects the pattern of dust spread by a dust storm, see how different types of soil behave in a dust storm, and then try to predict which regions are at greatest risk of dust storms. Let's get dusty!

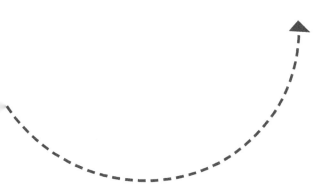

Tabletop Dust Storm

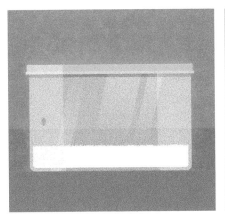 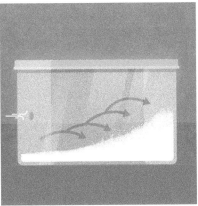 

QUICK QUERY

The Big Idea: Air seems like it's almost nothing at all, but it is strong enough to carry particles—and enough particles in the air create a dust storm. In this experiment, you'll make your own dust storm by blowing into a box full of flour. How does the path of the flour change if you blow softly or with more force? In what directions does the flour move?

 Cautions: Be careful not to breathe in any of the flour dust!

MATERIALS:

- ☐ **Flour**
- ☐ **Clear plastic box with a hole in one end**
- ☐ **Notebook or paper**
- ☐ **Pen or pencil**

continued >

THE STEPS:

1. Add a small amount of flour to the bottom of the clear box.

2. Blow into the hole in the box. Try making a gentle breeze first. Observe where the flour goes and how long the particles of flour stay suspended in the air. Record your observations.

3. Next, blow a big gust of wind into the box. Observe where the flour goes and how long the particles of flour stay in the air this time. Record your observations.

Observations: Did the particles of flour stay in the air longer with the big gust or with the gentle breeze? How were the scattering patterns of the dust different in the two types of wind?

The Hows and Whys: You probably noticed that the harder you blew on the flour, the more flour went into the air and the longer it stayed suspended there. This is also true of dust storms, where big gusts of wind pull tons of dust and sand into the sky.

KICK IT UP A NOTCH: **Try the experiment again, but angle your breath upward and downward to simulate updrafts and downdrafts. Will those change how long the particles are suspended in the air?**

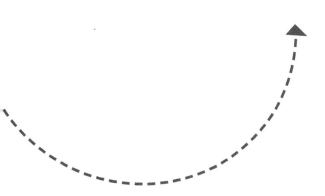

Dust Storm vs. Sandstorm

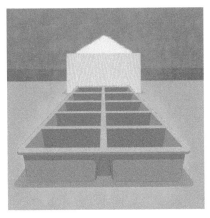

OBSERVATION DECK

The Big Idea: The soil on Earth's surface is different all over the world. How does each kind of soil behave in the wind? In this experiment, you'll see how dust (represented by powdered sugar), sand, and soil blow differently in the wind. Which do you think will blow farthest in the wind created by the hair dryer?

 Cautions: Ask a grown-up lab partner for help with plugging in and using the hair dryer.

MATERIALS:

☐ **Blocks of wood**

☐ **Ice-cube tray**

☐ **Sand**

☐ **Hair dryer**

☐ **Soil from the ground near your home**

☐ **Powdered sugar**

☐ **Pen or pencil**

continued >

THE STEPS:

1. Find a flat location near an electrical outlet. Make a small platform with the wooden blocks. Place the ice-cube tray a few inches in front of the platform. The platform should sit slightly higher than the top of the ice-cube tray.

2. Place a small pile of sand on the platform and plug in the hair dryer nearby.

3. Point the hair dryer at the pile of sand and toward the ice-cube tray. Turn on the hair dryer for about 5 to 10 seconds. Observe where in the ice-cube tray the sand lands.

4. Next, place a small pile of soil from the ground near your home on the platform. Perform the same procedure as in step 3. Observe where the soil ends up.

5. Then place a small pile of powdered sugar on the platform. Perform the same procedure as in step 3. Observe where the sugar ends up.

6. Look at the ice-cube tray and observe how each material traveled in the wind created by the hair dryer. Record your results in the data table that follows.

Observations: Which material traveled farthest in the wind? Which material spread into more of the ice-cube compartments?

The Hows and Whys: In a dust storm, the smallest, lightest particles are usually carried farthest by the wind—sometimes thousands of miles. If you look at the soil and the sand you used, you'll probably notice that whichever of the two had smaller particles ended up in the farthest ice-cube compartment.

KICK IT UP A NOTCH: **Try the same experiment with a variety of materials other than sand and soil. Try small pebbles, garden mulch, or any other material you're curious about.**

MATERIAL	NUMBER OF ICE-CUBE COMPARTMENTS WITH PARTICLES IN THEM AFTER USING THE HAIR DRYER
SAND	
SOIL	
POWDERED SUGAR	

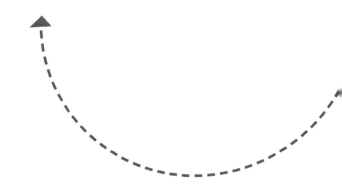

Mapping Dust Storms

The Big Idea: Dust storms are caused by a few specific geographic traits. Regions with very dry soil are the most likely to experience dust storms. In this experiment, you'll take a look at satellite images of Earth and try to find the regions that are most likely to have dust storms. What do you think those regions will look like in a satellite view? Then you'll do an internet search of regions prone to dust storms to check your predictions.

 Cautions: Have a grown-up lab partner help you with internet searches on the computer, tablet, or smartphone.

MATERIALS:

☐ **Computer, tablet, or smart-phone with access to satellite images of Earth and information on the geographic traits of different regions**

THE STEPS:

1. Look at a satellite image of Earth. Closely examine the color and makeup of each region you see. For example, does this region look mountainous? Is it mostly green, meaning it has lots of trees and vegetation?

2. Based on the appearance of the regions in the satellite image (and any additional research you've done), predict which regions might be prone to dust storms. Record your predictions in the data table here.

3. Do an internet search to see if dust storms are common in the regions you predicted.

Observations: What criteria did you use to decide whether or not a region would have dust storms? Were your predictions accurate?

The Hows and Whys: Generally, regions that have lots of dust storms are desert areas. In a satellite image, they would be wide-open spaces that appear to be a sort of tan or brown color from above. Areas that appear green and lush in a satellite image are usually full of plants and trees. Plants and trees have roots that dig into the soil, making it more difficult for the wind to pick up particles and carry them into the air.

KICK IT UP A NOTCH: **Does the region where you live experience a lot of dust storms? Look at the area around you and make a list of the things you think make your region prone to dust storms or dust storm proof.**

REGION	CRITERIA USED	RESEARCH: IS REGION ACTUALLY PRONE TO DUST STORMS?

PART THREE

NATURAL DISASTERS

CHAPTER 9

TORNADOES

A **tornado** is a spinning tube of air that extends from a thunderstorm cloud in the sky all the way down to the ground. The rotating winds of a tornado move very fast—sometimes more than 300 miles per hour. Tornado winds are very dangerous because they can pick up and throw debris. Just as you may have seen in the movie *The Wizard of Oz*, these winds are strong enough to pick up and destroy cars, trees, homes, and other buildings. Very powerful tornadoes have even destroyed entire towns.

Most tornadoes in the United States form in the Great Plains—a region that includes parts of North Dakota, South Dakota, Wyoming, Nebraska, Kansas, Colorado, Oklahoma, Texas, and New Mexico. Because this area experiences tornadoes so frequently, it is often called Tornado Alley.

Why are tornadoes so common in the Great Plains? In this region, cold, dry air from the north meets warm, moist air from the south. When the two air masses meet, clouds—and eventually thunderstorms—can form. Tornadoes result from specific kinds of thunderstorms. Tornadoes usually happen in the spring and summer. This is sometimes called tornado season.

How Does It Do That?

Tornadoes often form from spinning thunderstorms called supercells. But what exactly is a supercell, and how does it form a tornado? Let's find out!

1. **Supercells form in the same way as thunderstorms.** When warm air rises, creating an upward wind, or updraft, and cold air sinks, creating a downward wind, or downdraft, a supercell is formed.

2. **But supercells are different from average thunderstorms.** In a supercell, winds on the ground and winds much higher up blow in different directions, creating a rolling, horizontal tube of air. Next, the storm's updraft pulls the rolling tube of air upright. This movement creates a spinning thunderstorm, or supercell.

3. **Supercells are not very common.** But when they form, they can cause severe weather such as strong winds and hail—and occasionally tornadoes. Only about 30 percent of supercells form tornadoes.

4. **Tornadoes produce some of the fastest winds on Earth.** Some are a few feet wide, but others are wider than a football field. Tornadoes can last from several seconds to several hours.

5. **A meteorologist's job.** Meteorologists often don't know how fast or wide a tornado really was until they study the path of the damage after the storm. Were trees knocked over, while houses are still standing? Were small houses destroyed, but large buildings are untouched? After collecting this information, meteorologists can estimate the wind speeds of the storm and rate the tornado. Tornadoes are rated from 0 to 5 using the Enhanced Fujita Scale. An EF-0 tornado has wind speeds of about 65 to 85 miles per hour, while an EF-5 has wind speeds of 200 miles per hour or more.

6. **Tornado watch.** Meteorologists constantly keep an eye on the weather to see if conditions are right for a tornado. Pay attention to tornado warnings, updates, and guidance from your local weather experts.

POP CULTURE QUIZ!

One of the most popular weather movies of all time was the 1996 film *Twister*. As with most movies, while some events were based in fact, there were also many "do not try this at home" moments. Take this little true/false quiz to learn more about what is real and what is Hollywood storytelling.

People drive around in cars and trucks chasing tornadoes.

True! Many meteorologists and videographers flock to the Great Plains states in the spring and summer to chase storms. Some storm chasers come to do research and collect ground data, like the scientists in the film. Other storm chasers are mostly there to catch the wild storms on video. They then sell the videos and photos to television stations or post them on the internet.

You can hide from a tornado inside a car.

False! A character in the movie tries to seek shelter from a tornado inside a car. In real life, this would be a terrible idea. Tornado winds are so strong that they can pick up and throw a car, destroying the vehicle and seriously injuring any people inside. The best place to take shelter during a tornado is in the basement of a house or building. If you don't have a basement, take shelter in a room near the center of the house that doesn't have windows.

Tornado

WEATHER IN REAL LIFE

On March 3, 2019, a strong storm system caused about 40 tornadoes to tear through the southeastern United States. The tornadoes caused a great deal of damage in parts of Alabama, Florida, and Georgia.

One tornado that day was rated EF-4—meaning that there were winds of 166 miles per hour or more. This was the most dangerous tornado in the system. It left a miles-long trail of destroyed trees, homes, and other buildings. Because of just this one tornado, 23 people died and many others were injured.

After these storms, towns were completely destroyed. Although a disaster like a tornado is devastating, people in affected communities came together to clean up debris and help out their neighbors in need.

Disaster-relief workers and community volunteers loaded debris into garbage trucks to be hauled away. But cleanup is only one part of the process. Rebuilding takes a much longer time. Even a year after the storm, many people in affected communities still weren't able to move back to the exact places they used to call home.

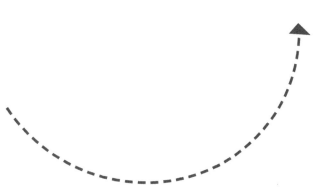

Get Involved!

In the experiments that follow, you'll learn how meteorologists determine the location of big storms, design a tornado-safe house, and plan a fire-safe garden. Let's get ready to (safely) learn about tornadoes!

Doppler Effect

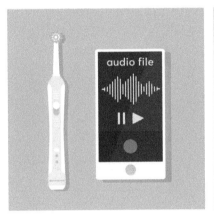 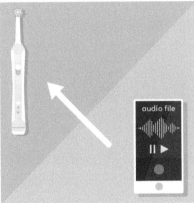 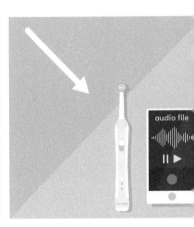

QUICK QUERY

The Big Idea: Meteorologists use Doppler radar to figure out the speed and direction of moving objects, such as thunderstorms. Doppler radar improves weather forecasts because it can determine the speed and direction of winds. In this experiment, you'll experience the Doppler effect using a toothbrush and an audio-recording device.

 Cautions: You may want to have a grown-up lab partner help you operate the electric toothbrush.

continued >

MATERIALS:

- ☐ **Battery-operated electric toothbrush**
- ☐ **Audio-recording device or app on a smartphone, tablet, or computer**

THE STEPS:

1. Turn on the toothbrush. Hold the toothbrush next to the microphone of your device, and record the sound. Do not move the toothbrush as you record.

2. Play the recording you just made to make sure it sounds the same as the original toothbrush sound.

3. Turn on the toothbrush a second time and press record on the audio-recording device or app. This time, move the toothbrush closer to and farther away from the microphone a few times.

4. Play the two recordings and observe how they are different.

Observations: How did the toothbrush sound when it was held still next to the microphone? How did its sound differ when you moved it toward and away from the microphone?

The Hows and Whys: The toothbrush sounds higher pitched as it moves toward the microphone and lower pitched as it moves away. This is because of a phenomenon called the Doppler effect. Sound is made up of waves. As an object making sound moves toward you, the waves are squeezed closer together. This makes the sound higher pitched. As the object moves away from you, the waves stretch out, resulting in a lower-pitched sound.

KICK IT UP A NOTCH: Try the experiment again, but this time move the toothbrush back and forth past the microphone quickly, then again slowly. Play the sound back for someone else. Can they tell how the movements were different based only on the sounds?

Keep the Outside from Getting In

TAKE IT OUTSIDE

The Big Idea: Tornadoes have very high wind speeds, which can cause damage to houses and buildings. Engineers and architects can take steps to design tornado-safe rooms and buildings. Grab a pencil and paper (or a computer drawing program) and design a tornado-safe room of your own. Here are a few tornado-safe features:

1. The room should have no windows.

2. The room should not be prone to flooding.

3. The walls and ceiling should be safe from wind and debris flying at up to 250 miles per hour.

4. The door should open into the room so that you can still open it even if the floor outside is blocked by debris.

5. The room should have a strong foundation.

 Cautions: None! This activity is safe for all ages.

MATERIALS:

☐ **Pencil**　　　　　　　☐ **Paper**

continued >

THE STEPS:

1. Read the list of features needed for a tornado-safe building on the previous page.

2. Use a pencil and paper to design a house or building of any kind that would be safe to shelter in during a tornado.

Observations: What features were needed to make the building safe during a tornado? Was it difficult to add these features while also making sure there were bathrooms, bedrooms, and all the other normal parts of a house?

The Hows and Whys: Tornadoes bring with them strong winds, intense rains, and sometimes even hail. The best place to be safe from tornadoes is in a basement—and one that isn't at risk of flooding. The next best option is a room near the center of a house without any windows. Think about your own house and where you might go during a tornado or other extreme storm.

KICK IT UP A NOTCH: Try actually building your design with plastic building blocks. Is your design safe—and still livable?

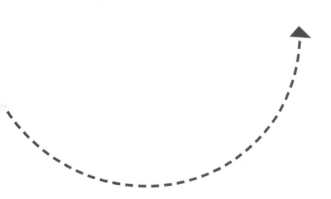

Flowers to Prevent a Fire

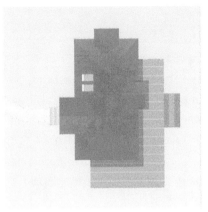  

TAKE IT OUTSIDE

The Big Idea: Tornadoes can start fires, and their ferocious winds can carry this fire well outside the path of a tornado. Although you can't stop the winds that cause fire to spread, you can help make your home safer from fires. In this experiment, you'll plan a fire-safe flower bed and garden that will surround a house. Aside from choosing the right plants, what could you do to make a garden safer from fires?

Here are a few fire-safe plants you can include in your garden:

1. Moss phlox
2. Nannyberry
3. Columbine

4. Bearberry
5. Wintergreen
6. Wild geranium

 Cautions: None! This activity is safe for all ages.

MATERIALS:

☐ **Paper**

☐ **Pen or pencil**

continued >

THE STEPS:

1. Use the paper and pen or pencil to draw a bird's-eye view of a house or apartment building.

2. Draw flower beds with fire-safe plants and other fire-resistant features surrounding the house or apartment building. Try to make the features something that people living in the building would enjoy—while also keeping the building safe from fires.

Observations: What did you take into consideration when designing the garden? Was it easier or more difficult than you expected?

The Hows and Whys: As people moved into the wilderness to build neighborhoods and houses, they brought with them the plants and flowers they remembered from the places they used to live. Having plants you like isn't a problem, but bringing in plants that aren't native to a region can be. In general, hot, dry climates can only support certain kinds of plants. If you bring in non-native species, they may dry out quickly, creating a fire hazard.

KICK IT UP A NOTCH: Visit some local gardens in your town. Do you see any that appear to be fire safe? Do you see any that seem to need work when it comes to fire safety? If you notice anything in your own gardens that could be improved, talk to your parents about what changes you would make and why.

CHAPTER 10

HURRICANES

Hurricanes are some of the strongest and most recognizable storms on Earth. From above, a hurricane looks like a spinning pinwheel with a hole in the middle. However, from the ground they're quite scary. With wind speeds of up to 200 miles per hour, these violent storms can destroy houses and rip trees right out of the ground. They are also huge, often measuring about 300 miles across.

These giant storms begin as thunderstorms just north or south of the equator. Why there? The warm, tropical water creates moisture and heat that fuel the storm. Hurricanes usually form in tropical climates, such as off the western coast of Africa or in the Caribbean Sea. A hurricane can form at any time of year if the conditions are right, but most hurricanes in the Atlantic happen from June to November. So that time of year is called hurricane season.

Where do hurricanes never form? Hurricanes can't form right at the equator. They also rarely form off the coasts of Europe or off the West Coast of the United States.

How Does It Do That?

1. **Hurricanes begin over warm ocean waters.** The tropical waters just north and south of the equator create warm, moist air that rises into the atmosphere. As we learned in previous chapters, water vapor cools as it rises, becoming water droplets that form clouds.

2. **The clouds grow bigger.** With the warm, moist air continuing to rise off the ocean, clouds grow bigger and bigger, forming thunderstorm clouds. Many thunderstorm clouds form just north and south of the equator. But how do thunderstorm clouds turn into a spinning hurricane?

3. **The rotation of the storms is an effect of Earth's rotation.** Because Earth always spins in the same direction, winds—and other things traveling in straight lines—begin to veer in one direction. Winds in the Northern Hemisphere tend to turn toward the right, and those in the Southern Hemisphere turn toward the left.

4. **The Coriolis effect.** As we learned earlier, in chapter 2, this is called the Coriolis effect, and it's what turns a cluster of thunderstorm clouds into a spinning hurricane. Because of the Coriolis effect, hurricanes in the Northern Hemisphere rotate counterclockwise. Hurricanes in the Southern Hemisphere, on the other hand, rotate clockwise.

5. **The need for speed.** Once the wind speeds in this rotating storm reach 39 miles per hour, meteorologists call it a tropical storm. And once the storm reaches 74 miles per hour, it is called a hurricane.

6. **The eye of the storm.** In the center of a hurricane is an area of relative calm called the eye. The eye is an area of low air pressure with calm winds and no rain. However, just outside the eye is the eye wall. The eye wall is far from calm—it has some of the storm's strongest winds. Spiraling out from the eye wall are bands of thunderstorms called rain bands.

7. **Gaining strength.** A hurricane picks up its energy from the warm, moist air over the tropical ocean water. As long as the storm stays over warm water, its winds will continue to get stronger. Storms begin to lose their strength once they encounter colder waters. A hurricane

also starts to weaken when it encounters land. However, it is still very powerful. Wind and rain from hurricanes are very destructive and can damage or destroy houses and other buildings in their paths.

8. **Dangerous storm surges.** Storm surge occurs when the level of the ocean rises abnormally high because of the storm's winds and movement. Some hurricanes produce storm surges higher than 25 feet. Sometimes the flooding from storm surge ends up causing more damage than the hurricane itself.

9. **More hurricanes in our future?** Scientists have observed how hurricanes are changing as our planet undergoes climate change. They predict that as Earth warms, hurricanes will become more intense—and the number of intense hurricanes will increase. Rising sea levels are another result of climate change. So scientists predict that these higher seas will also cause more intense flooding during hurricanes.

CYCLONE, TYPHOON, OR HURRICANE?

You've probably heard of big hurricanes hitting islands in the Caribbean or the coast of Florida, but did you know these big storms happen in tropical areas all over the world? It's true! However, they have different names depending on where they happen.

For example, if the storm happens in the North Atlantic Ocean or eastern Pacific Ocean, it's a hurricane. But if the same type of storm happens in the South Atlantic Ocean or Indian Ocean, it's called a **tropical cyclone**. Ever heard of a **typhoon**? That is a hurricane-like storm occurring in the western Pacific Ocean.

WEATHER IN REAL LIFE

The 2017 Atlantic hurricane season set lots of records—and not in a good way. The ocean waters were especially warm that year, fueling many hurricanes. In fact, it was the most active hurricane season in US history, and the most expensive.

Four major hurricanes caused a lot of the damage that year. The hurricanes were named Harvey, Irma, Maria, and Nate. Hurricane Harvey hit the coast of Texas in August of 2017 with 100 mph winds and up to five feet of rain, which caused major flooding.

A few weeks later, Hurricane Irma hit land in Florida and the Virgin Islands, causing lots of damage and leaving about 16 million people without electricity. Later, Hurricane Maria devastated Puerto Rico. Three months after the hurricane hit, more than half of the island still didn't have electrical power.

Then, in October, Hurricane Nate arrived on land in Central America and the United States, causing hundreds of millions of dollars in damage.

How long did it take to recover from these storms? It can take years to rebuild communities after major storms like these. Electricity and roads can sometimes be restored within weeks or months. However, it has taken people in affected regions—such as Texas and Puerto Rico—several years to clean up the debris and begin repairing and rebuilding houses.

Get Involved!

Hurricanes are dangerous storms, but we can learn more about them by safely doing experiments at home. In this chapter, we'll create a tool to monitor wind speeds, study the effects of storm surge, and track real storms over the ocean. Take a look at the materials lists to make sure you have everything you need, and let's get started!

Wind Spinner

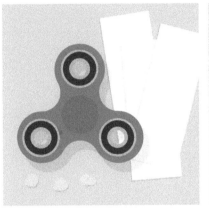 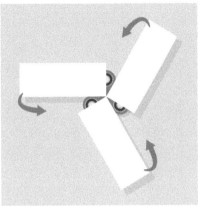 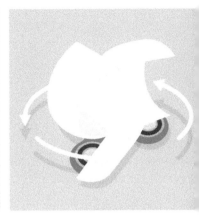

QUICK QUERY

The Big Idea: Meteorologists use tools called anemometers to measure wind speed and direction from the ground. These tools help in studying many different types of weather. However, they can be especially helpful in determining how strong a hurricane is and where it's traveling. In this experiment, you'll use the spinning action of a fidget spinner toy and some sails made from paper and tape. What location near your house do you think will have the strongest wind?

 Cautions: Be careful when using scissors.

MATERIALS:

- ☐ **Ruler**
- ☐ **Paper**
- ☐ **Scissors**
- ☐ **Tape or poster putty**
- ☐ **Fidget spinner**

continued >

THE STEPS:

1. Using the ruler, measure out three sails on your paper. Each sail should be a rectangle 2 inches by 4 inches. Using your scissors, cut out each sail.

2. Place the paper rectangles so that the short sides are at the bottom and top. Label the corners of each rectangle with the numbers 1 through 4; start with the number 1 in the bottom left corner and go counterclockwise.

3. Place the corner labeled 1 in the center of the fidget spinner while pushing the area between 1 and 2 into the putty. Do this for all three rectangles.

4. Lift up each of the corners labeled 4. Stack the number 4's on top of one another with the corners of the paper pointing to the middle of the fidget spinner. Use tape to join the corners together in this way. Corners labeled 3 should be free and pointing to the outside of the fidget spinner.

5. Blow air into the sails or set the device outside in the wind to test it.

Observations: What did you notice when you placed your anemometer in the wind?

The Hows and Whys: This type of anemometer works by catching the wind in the sails, which turns the fidget spinner. You can use this simple design to make a relative measurement of the wind. If the fidget spinner is moving fast, the winds are at higher speeds than when it is spinning slowly. However, if you wanted to know the exact wind speed, you'd need to do some special calculations based on the size of the fidget spinner.

KICK IT UP A NOTCH: **Once you've made your anemometer, test wind speeds in several spots near your home. Do any areas act as wind tunnels, funneling the wind into one spot? Are there any areas where the wind is completely blocked?**

The Big Wave

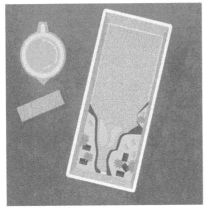  

OBSERVATION DECK

The Big Idea: A storm surge is a giant mass of water that comes ashore during a hurricane. This flood of water can cause a great deal of the damage from the storm. In this experiment, you'll create your own storm surge in a plastic tub indoors. When you create the wind, which area of the tub do you think will receive the most damage?

MATERIALS:

- ☐ **1 bag (40 to 50 pounds) play sand**
- ☐ **Large, low-sided plastic container, like an under-the-bed storage bin**
- ☐ **Water**
- ☐ **Sponges**
- ☐ **Items to represent houses**
- ☐ **Tiny toy animals, people, and cars**
- ☐ **Plastic straws**
- ☐ **Erasable markers**
- ☐ **Block of wood or a large, firm poster board (something to make waves with)**
- ☐ **Paper towels**

THE STEPS:

1. Place sand in one half of the long plastic container. The sand will represent land.

2. Slightly moisten the sand with water. Use a finger to create a curvy river down the

continued >

center of the sand. As the river gets closer to the part that will be the ocean, you can create several smaller curvy rivers branching off.

3. On the sides of the river, create low areas in the sand. Place pieces of damp sponge in these areas, which will represent salt marshes. You can also create marshes—grassy wetlands—away from the ocean area.

4. Using moistened sand, create an oval-shaped island several inches away from the mouth of your river in the ocean area. The island should not block the mouth of the river.

5. Add water slowly to the ocean side of the container. Add enough water so that the island

is surrounded and the mouth of the river contains some water.

6. Add houses, animals, people, and cars to the island and along the river. You can use plastic straws to place houses on stilts.

7. On the outside of the container, use an erasable marker to place a mark every half inch from the edge of the ocean to the end of the land. Number each mark starting with 0, then 1, 2, 3, etc.

8. If using a block of wood, gently tap the water in the ocean by moving the block up and down to create mild waves. If using firm poster board, wave it up and down near the water to make gentle waves. Use the paper towels if any water spills.

9. Observe what happens.

Observations: What happens to your island, the marshes, and the land behind the island? What happens to the people, cars, animals, and houses?

The Hows and Whys: Building barrier islands—like the oval island you created in this exercise—is a way that we can prevent storm surges from destroying a coastal community. Grassy marshes—represented by the sponges in this experiment—can absorb energy and reduce the height of waves.

KICK IT UP A NOTCH: Try creating bigger waves by moving the block up and down faster or use a hair dryer or fan to represent wind. Try creating more islands or more marshes. What happens if the island is farther away from the mainland?

Track a Hurricane

The Big Idea: Hurricane season in North America happens every summer as tropical storms pick up speed from warm oceans, with some eventually turning into hurricanes. In this experiment, you'll follow news reports of tropical storms and try to predict which ones will become hurricanes. Which factors do you think will fuel and strengthen a tropical storm?

> **Cautions:** Always check with an adult lab partner before using the internet.

MATERIALS:

- ☐ **TV or computer with internet access to track tropical storms**
- ☐ **Pen or pencil**

THE STEPS:

1. Watch the news on TV or use the internet to find out what tropical storms are forming in the Atlantic Ocean.

2. Track each tropical storm every day and record its location, wind speed, ocean temperature, etc. in the data table that follows.

continued >

3. Make a prediction whether each tropical storm will become a hurricane or not. Write down your predictions.

4. Record whether each tropical storm turned into a hurricane or not in the data table.

Observations: What factors were important for a tropical storm to become a hurricane? Wind speed? Ocean temperature?

The Hows and Whys: Meteorologists use satellite images to track where tropical storms are, but they also use wind speed and direction measurements in the middle of the atmosphere to determine which way the storm will move and how fast it's moving. This generally allows them to get a good idea of where the storm will go. However, storms can also be unpredictable, so don't feel bad if it takes some time to perfect your predictions.

KICK IT UP A NOTCH: Look back at records of tropical storms that turned into hurricanes in previous years. Use this information to help you make your predictions.

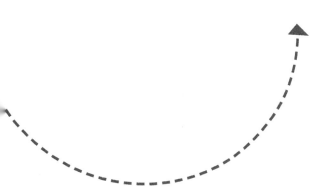

TROPICAL STORM NAME	LOCATION	WIND SPEED	OCEAN TEMPER-ATURE	PREDICTION: HURRICANE OR NO?	RESULT: HURRICANE OR NO?

CHAPTER 11

ICE STORMS

You look out the window on a cold, gray day. You notice that there is precipitation, but it's not quite snow and not quite rain. After a little while, it appears that your window is coated in a thin layer of crystal-clear ice. Have you ever experienced this phenomenon? If so, you've probably just seen an **ice storm**!

An ice storm refers to the weather conditions that result in about a quarter inch of ice—or more—accumulating on the ground, houses, cars, and anything else outside in the area of the storm. With the right atmospheric conditions, ice storms can happen almost anywhere. However, in the United States they are most common in the Northeast.

Although a quarter inch of ice may not seem like much of a natural disaster, this small amount can cause a lot of damage. Even a light layer of ice can cause car accidents on slippery streets. If there's a bit more, the weight of these layers of ice can make electrical lines fall down, causing widespread power outages.

How Does It Do That?

An ice storm is a strange mixture of a snowstorm and a rain shower. Here's how it works:

1. **Ice storms begin in the clouds.** Ice storms start when warm water vapor in the air rises high into the atmosphere, forming a cloud. But instead of the water in the cloud falling as rain or snow, it sort of falls as both.

2. **An ice storm cloud is made of ice crystals.** As the tiny ice crystals begin to clump together, they get heavier, falling out of the cloud as snowflakes. As the snow falls, it passes through a layer of warm air. This warmer part of the atmosphere causes the snowflake to melt into rain. As the newly formed raindrop continues to fall, it encounters a below-freezing layer of air near the ground.

3. **Sleet or freezing rain?** If the rain freezes in the air before it hits the ground, it becomes sleet—a chunky mixture of ice and rain. However, if the rain doesn't freeze in the air, the water becomes supercooled. This means that, even though it's below freezing temperature, the water is still a liquid, but it becomes frozen ice as soon as it comes into contact with a surface. This is freezing rain, and that is what causes an ice storm.

4. **Freezing rain can make the environment look beautiful.** When everything is covered with a layer of ice, it looks like a glittering winter wonderland! But don't be fooled: An ice storm can be very dangerous. Even a layer of ice only a tenth of an inch thick can make roads feel like skating rinks, causing cars to slide past Stop signs or right off the road. As thicker layers of ice begin to accumulate, the weight of the ice becomes substantial.

5. **Heavy layers of ice can cause a lot of trouble.** Ice on tree branches make them 30 percent heavier—and can add up to 500 pounds of weight to power lines—made even worse by gusty winds. This can cause tree branches to break off and fall onto houses and into streets. Power lines can become so heavy that lines snap, causing widespread power outages that can be extremely dangerous, especially in winter. In subzero temperatures, people who lose electricity may have no other way to heat their homes—leading to dangerously low temperatures even indoors.

6. **What's in store for the future?** As Earth's climate changes, evidence suggests that extreme weather will become more commonplace than ever. Devastating ice storms may become more frequent in parts of the United States and Canada as the planet warms.

POP CULTURE QUIZ!

In Disney's movie *Frozen*, Princess Elsa has a superpower: She can create ice and snow whenever and wherever she wants. She can use her powers to play—like to build a snowman. At one point in the movie, she even builds a giant ice castle to live in.

Now, I think we all know that this movie isn't exactly based on fact, but let's see how Elsa's powers in *Frozen* stack up to a real ice storm with this short movie quiz!

True or False: Ice storms are caused by people with magical powers who can shoot icy wind out of their hands.

False! (I hope this one was pretty easy.) In real life, there is no person who can control weather events—including ice storms—on demand. So what really causes an ice storm? Ice storms are generally caused by freezing rain. This happens naturally, based on conditions in the atmosphere—no magical powers required!

True or False: When Princess Anna meets Olaf the snowman for the first time in an icy forest, they are surrounded by ice-covered branches hanging down from trees. This can happen in real life, too.

Ice Storm

True! When an ice storm rolls through town, freezing rain covers almost every surface—including tree branches—in a clear glaze of ice. The trees in the forest in *Frozen* have droopy branches, much like a weeping willow tree. Check out how the movie compares to this picture of ice-covered branches in real life.

WEATHER IN REAL LIFE

One of the worst ice storms in US history happened in parts of New England, New York, and southern Canada in January 1998. Why was this storm so devastating? The ice from this storm accumulated to three inches thick, causing lots of damage—including power outages for millions of people in the region. Icy streets, as well as fallen branches and power lines, made transportation extremely difficult.

Fixing all of the damage caused by this ice storm cost billions of dollars. And in the United States and Canada combined, the ice storm caused more than 40 people to die, while over 1,000 more were injured.

It took crews several weeks to repair power lines and restore electricity to the communities hit hardest by the storm. However, the damage to the nearby forests took much longer to repair. The ice storm killed or severely damaged up to 20 percent of the trees in the region, and many more had light to moderate damage.

Get Involved!

What's the best way to de-ice a sidewalk? How does ice bring down a power line? Can rain really freeze in the air? Answer these questions and more with the experiments that are up next!

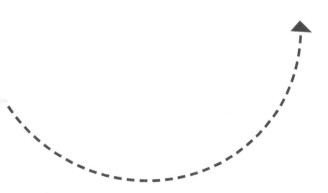

Icy Sidewalk

QUICK QUERY

The Big Idea: In an ice storm, sidewalks and roads are covered with ice and are unsafe for driving and walking. Cities and towns typically use salt to help melt the ice, but is that the best choice we have? In this experiment, you'll try a variety of substances to test what works best in an ice storm.

> **Cautions:** Clean up any water from melting ice immediately so that you don't slip.

MATERIALS:

- ☐ Ice cubes
- ☐ Rimmed baking pan or plastic box
- ☐ Salt
- ☐ Clock, stopwatch, or timer app on a smartphone or tablet
- ☐ Pen or pencil
- ☐ Sugar
- ☐ Beet juice
- ☐ Pickle juice

continued >

THE STEPS:

1. Place the ice cubes in the rimmed baking pan or plastic box.

2. Sprinkle the salt over the ice cubes.

3. Using the clock, stopwatch, or timer app, time how long it takes for half of the ice to melt. Record the time on the table that follows using a pen or pencil.

4. Repeat steps 1 to 3 using sugar, beet juice, and pickle juice in place of salt. Then repeat steps 1 to 3 using a mixture of beet juice and salt.

Observations: Did the salt, sugar, beet juice, pickle juice, or salty beet juice cause the ice to melt fastest?

The Hows and Whys: Salt has been used to de-ice roads and sidewalks for decades. Pickle juice also has salt in it, so it may have the same effect. What about the other substances? Sugar probably won't have much effect, nor will beet juice on its own. But beet juice mixed with salt will make a sticky mixture that melts the ice all over. This is a formula sometimes used on roads.

KICK IT UP A NOTCH: **What other substances could you use to melt ice? Try them out.**

SUBSTANCE	TIME FOR HALF OF ICE TO MELT
SALT	
SUGAR	
BEET JUICE	
PICKLE JUICE	
SALTY BEET JUICE	

Weighty Ice

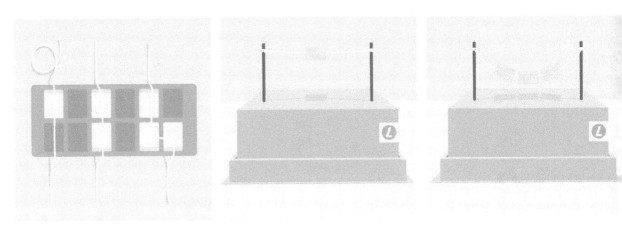

The Big Idea: Ice storms can be dangerous for many reasons, including downed power lines. Here, you'll learn why ice storms bring down power lines while rain does not. How many ice cubes do you think you would need to weigh down your model power line?

Cautions: Have a grown-up lab partner poke holes in the shoebox.

MATERIALS:

- ☐ **3 pieces of string or shoelaces**
- ☐ **Ice-cube tray**
- ☐ **Water**
- ☐ **Shoebox**
- ☐ **Chopsticks**

THE STEPS:

1. Place one of the strings or shoelaces in the ice-cube tray so that its center is in one ice-cube compartment. Fill that one compartment with water. Place the second string or shoelace so that its center is in two ice-cube compartments and fill those two compartments with water. Place the third string or shoelace so that its center is in three ice-cube compartments and pour water into those three compartments.

continued >

2. Place the ice-cube tray with the strings in it in the freezer until the water freezes and forms ice cubes.

3. While the water is freezing in the ice-cube trays, set the shoebox upside down and poke holes in the bottom. These will hold your "poles" (chopsticks).

4. When the ice cubes on the strings are frozen, start with the one-ice-cube string and attach an end of the string to each chopstick. Put the other end of each chopstick into a hole in the box.

5. See which string of ice cubes (one ice cube, two ice cubes, or three ice cubes) is needed to weigh down the chopsticks and string.

Observations: What happened as you added more ice cubes? At what point did the chopsticks fall over?

The Hows and Whys: Ice weighs much more than water, so an ice storm does much more damage to power lines and trees than rainwater. Eventually, the ice becomes so heavy that the line will snap, or the poles that hold the power line will topple over.

KICK IT UP A NOTCH: Design a better power line. What design would you use to keep the power line from sagging in an ice storm?

- -

Frozen Bubbles

TAKE IT OUTSIDE

The Big Idea: Ice doesn't need to fall out of the sky to be dangerous. On very cold days, even a small amount of rain can create an instantaneous, slippery ice mat. In this experiment, you'll see just how quickly ice can freeze in the form of a bubble. What do you think will happen if the bubble freezes before it reaches the ground?

 Cautions: Always wear cold-weather clothing when going outside on below-freezing days!

Note: I know that not everyone lives in a climate where days get this cold in the winter. Unfortunately, this experiment won't work at higher temperatures. If you have this problem, and you know someone who lives in a cold enough climate, maybe they can do the experiment with you over video chat.

MATERIALS:

- ☐ **Very cold weather, such as 10°F (−23°C) or colder**
- ☐ **Bubble liquid**
- ☐ **Bubble wand**

continued >

THE STEPS:

1. Dress appropriately to be outside in temperatures below freezing. Take the bubble liquid and wand outside.

2. Dip the bubble wand in the bubble liquid and blow a bubble. Blow the bubble up into the air.

3. Observe whether the bubble freezes and what happens to it when it reaches the ground.

Observations: Did the bubble freeze? Why or why not? What happens when a frozen bubble reaches the ground?

The Hows and Whys: Freezing rain is caused by water droplets that fall and become supercooled in a cold layer of air near the ground—eventually freezing on a surface. In this experiment, the bubble works a bit like freezing rain—freezing in the cold air just above the ground.

> **KICK IT UP A NOTCH:** What happens if you blow bubbles of different sizes? How long does it take different-size bubbles to freeze? What happens when the bubbles fall to the ground from different heights?

FAIR WEATHER TO YOU!

Understanding how our atmosphere works to create the weather we experience every day is no easy task. I know you won't understand it all even after reading this book and following along with the experiments, but I hope this will be a jumping-off point for your own curiosity. Maybe you'll ask some new questions and answer them by designing your own experiments!

Whether you decide to become a meteorologist or an artist or a chef when you grow up, the weather will always be a part of your life. And now you'll know a lot more about why things are the way they are.

Thank you for learning with me, and I hope you enjoy the rest of your journey into the world of weather!

GLOSSARY

advection fog: A type of fog that forms when warm air meets a cool surface

aerosols: Tiny particles such as smoke, pollen, and dust that float around in the atmosphere

air pressure: The weight of the molecules in the air pushing down on Earth's surface

atmosphere: The layers of gases and particles that surround Earth

avalanche: A mass of snow that slides down a mountain

barometer: An instrument used to detect local changes in air pressure

climate: The average weather conditions in a region over decades, centuries, or even longer

climate change: A significant change in the average weather conditions—temperature, rainfall, etc.—in a place over decades, centuries, or more

cold front: The changeover region where a mass of cold air moves toward, and then slides underneath, a mass of warm air, thrusting the warm air higher in the atmosphere

condensation: The process by which a gas turns into a liquid

convection: Movement in a gas or liquid in which the warmer parts rise and the colder parts sink

Coriolis effect: An interaction between the atmosphere and Earth's rotation on its axis, causing winds in the Northern Hemisphere to bend toward the right, and the winds in the Southern Hemisphere to bend toward the left

downdraft: An air current that moves downward in the atmosphere as cold air sinks

drought: An event that occurs when a region gets much less rain than usual over a long period of time, often leading to decreased water supply

dust storm: An event that occurs when winds are so strong that they pick up and blow particles of soil into the atmosphere, eventually dropping the soil particles somewhere else

evaporation: The process by which a liquid turns into a gas

flash flood: An event with heavy rain when waters rise so fast that buildings can flood and people can get caught off guard; common in urban areas with many paved surfaces

glacier: A natural ice formation made up of snow that piles up over many years, with each new layer of snow pressing down on the layer beneath it

global warming: An increase in the average temperature of Earth's surface, oceans, and atmosphere caused by increased amounts of greenhouse gases in the atmosphere

greenhouse effect: The process by which gases in Earth's atmosphere trap some of the Sun's heat, causing the planet to be warmer

greenhouse gases: Heat-trapping gases in the atmosphere, including water vapor, carbon dioxide, and methane

gust front: A line of gusty winds created by certain weather conditions

humidity: The amount of water vapor in the air

hurricane: A spinning storm with fast winds that happens above warm waters in the North Atlantic Ocean or eastern Pacific Ocean

hypothesis: In a scientific experiment, a hypothesis is a testable idea about why something happens the way it does

ice fog: A type of fog that occurs in extremely cold air temperatures when water vapor freezes into small ice crystals instead of condensing into water droplets

ice storm: The weather conditions that result in about a quarter inch of ice—or more—accumulating on ground, houses, cars, and anything else outside in the area

jet stream: A band of extremely fast-moving wind high up in the atmosphere

meteorology: The field of science that involves studying our atmosphere, how it changes, and how it affects our weather

monsoon: An extreme rain that happens in India and nearby regions when the Sun heats the ocean and the land unevenly

natural disaster: A terrible event in nature that results in serious damage to property—including houses, roads, or even entire cities—and often in many deaths, completely changing the lives of people who live nearby

precipitation: The result of water vapor in the atmosphere condensing and falling from the clouds, such as rain or snow

radiation fog: A type of fog that forms when moist air approaches the cool ground, causing condensation (the formation of water droplets) in the air—just like a cloud

scientific method: The organized process that scientists use to answer questions about the natural world and how it works

snow cornice: A formation that occurs when snow is blown by the wind at the sharp edge of a ridge or cliff face, creating a ledge of snow and ice

snow penitentes: Spikes of snow that become compacted by certain melting and evaporation patterns

steam fog: A type of fog that forms over the tops of lakes, usually in the fall and winter seasons

supercell: An unusually large, rotating thunderstorm

tornado: A spinning tube of air that extends from a thunderstorm cloud in the sky all the way down to the ground

tropical cyclone: A spinning storm with fast winds that happens above warm waters in the South Atlantic Ocean or Indian Ocean

typhoon: A spinning storm with fast winds that happens above warm waters in the western Pacific Ocean

updraft: An air current that moves upward in the atmosphere as warm air rises

valley fog: A type of fog that forms in mountainous areas, usually at night, filling the valleys between mountains

warm front: The changeover region where a warm air mass is replacing a cold air mass in the atmosphere

water cycle: The movement of water on Earth from the soil and oceans to clouds, then to precipitation, then back to the soil and oceans

water vapor: The gas form of water

weather: A description of the conditions in Earth's atmosphere at a certain place and time

weather phenomenon: A weather event, whether it is as routine as a light rainstorm or as extreme as a hurricane

weather satellite: A machine that orbits high above Earth, collecting information about the temperature, gases, water vapor, and clouds in our atmosphere

weather station: A setup of several different types of instruments that constantly collect information about the weather in a specific area

wildfire: An uncontrolled fire that is fueled by vegetation such as plants and trees

wind: Air movement caused by differences in air temperature and pressure

RESOURCES

DK Find Out: Weather: DKFindOut.com/us/earth/weather
This website has some great explanations of everyday and extreme weather events. If you learn better from visual explanations, this website has some awesome diagrams that draw out exactly how things work.

National Geographic: NationalGeographic.com
National Geographic has a ton of great reference pages about the weather phenomena we discussed in this book and many more, including the latest news.

National Geographic Kids: Climate Change: Kids.NationalGeographic.com /explore/science/climate-change
Want to learn more about how Earth's climate is changing—and what that could mean for our weather in the near future? This page is a great introduction to the effects of Earth's warming climate.

National Geographic Kids: Everything Weather by Kathy Furgang
If you want to load up on weather facts to stump your family and friends, this book is a great place to start! There are also lots of amazing photographs that will really spark wonder.

National Severe Storms Laboratory: Severe Weather 101: NSSL.NOAA .gov/education/svrwx101
Want to learn more about severe weather such as tornadoes and hurricanes? Check out the articles and latest research here!

National Weather Service: JetStream—An Online School for Weather: Weather.gov/jetstream
The National Weather Service, which is responsible for monitoring and forecasting the weather in the United States, offers a great online "weather school" with everything you could ever want to know about the weather that affects our lives. Check it out if you want to take a deep dive into what makes our atmosphere tick!

PBS LearningMedia: Earth and Space Science: PBSLearningMedia.org
/subjects/science/earth-and-space-science/weather-and-climate
Want to suggest some cool weather and climate lessons for your teachers and classmates? Take a look at the lessons and activities offered by PBS LearningMedia.

Smithsonian Weather Lab: SSEC.SI.edu/weather-lab
Meteorologists create models to predict what will happen next in our weather. You can use the Smithsonian Weather Lab to learn to make these predictions, too! While you're there, you can check out their weather games as well.

Space Weather Center: SpaceWeatherCenter.org
Did you know that Earth also experiences weather from the Sun? This weather is called space weather, and if it's extreme, it can cause all kinds of problems here on Earth, such as power outages. Check out this page to learn more!

Weather Wiz Kids: WeatherWizKids.com
Designed by a meteorologist, Weather Wiz Kids is a good resource for kid-friendly information about weather as well as more experiments you can do to explore weather concepts indoors and out.

NOTES

Write your weather observations and experiment notes here.

NOTES

Write your weather observations and experiment notes here.

NOTES

Write your weather observations and experiment notes here.

NOTES

Write your weather observations and experiment notes here.

NOTES

Write your weather observations and experiment notes here.

INDEX

ACKNOWLEDGMENTS

Thank you to the thousands of meteorologists and scientists who work very hard to understand our atmosphere and changing climate. Thanks also to the science journalists, writers, and educators who work (just as hard) to translate this cutting-edge science for the rest of us.

And thanks most of all to my brilliantly kind and patient husband, Tim. You cared for our small children all by yourself for many weekends so that I could shut myself in a room and write this book. And you did it all while social distancing during a global pandemic. This was a herculean task, and I'm so grateful that we're on the same team!

ABOUT THE AUTHOR

 **Jessica Stoller-Conrad** is a science writer specializing in content for young audiences. In her most recent role, she produces digital content that explains space and Earth science for kids. Previously, she wrote for a variety of news outlets and institutions covering biology, engineering, health, and food. Jessica holds a master's degree in biological sciences from the University of Notre Dame. She lives with her husband and their two sons in Southern California.

CPSIA information can be obtained
at www.ICGtesting.com
Printed in the USA
JSHW051104141021
19558JS00001B/10